THE SEARCH FOR
LOST ORIGINS

THE SEARCH FOR LOST ORIGINS

A Collection of Reports on Today's Breakthrough Research

FROM THE EDITORS OF ATLANTIS RISING MAGAZINE

ATLANTIS RISING
BOOKS
Livingston, Montana

CONTENTS

To the growing number of true scientists and scholars willing to risk their prestige, perks and privileges for the sake of something as ephemeral as the truth.

Introduction

When *Atlantis Rising Magazine* was launched in the fall of 1994, we stated the following:

"Most new-age publications focus strongly on holistic health and life-style matters, and well they should. If the 'new age' is not about developing a higher understanding of the human body and its relationship to the world, then what is it, anyway? So we agree with the preeminent importance of holistic health issues and we intend to give them plenty of quality space in this publication.

"Having said that, though, it seemed to us that a couple areas very much neglected by most magazines with similar demographic intent were ancient mysteries and future science. We were at a loss to explain why. Here were two subjects which, by virtue of their broad appeal, have a greater potential to attract a large following to the new-age banner than yoga or vegetarianism ever could.

"Sadly, it appeared, that both ancient mysteries and future science have, in fact, been co-opted by those notorious crowd chasers, the tabloid press. In the meantime, those with serious aspirations to raise the planetary consciousness seemed to find such matters somehow beneath them—choosing instead to concentrate on more rarefied concerns. The curious public is left to choose between interesting material presented without credibility or boring material presented in an apparently credible way.

An unhappy state of affairs, indeed.

"The public's growing fascination with the hidden secrets of our ancient origins and the extraordinary possibilities of our future is an open door to the kind of universal consciousness-raising that all of us hope to see in a dawning 'new age.' Besides, we at 'Atlantis Rising' share that fascination, and we can think of nothing we would rather do than cater to it. We do believe, however, that it is entirely possible to cover such areas with dignity and credibility, while avoiding the sin of becoming bland or boring."

So far, we have stuck by our guns, and, in the process, produced an exciting array of material unavailable from any other single source. So, it occurred, that the time had come to make that material available in book form.

The present volume concentrates on ancient mysteries, but future titles will focus on breakthrough science, visions from the beyond, and the other hot topics that have made "Atlantis Rising" the unique publication it is.

PART ONE
FOOTPRINTS
IN THE SAND

1
O.O.P.s
Out-of-Place Artifacts
by Dr. Joseph Jochmans, Litt.D.

Walk into any modern museum, or open any history text-
book, and the picture of the past presented is one in
which humanity started from primitive beginnings, and steadily
progressed upward in the development of culture and science.
Most of the artifacts preserved in archaeological and geological
records have been neatly arranged to fit this "accepted" linear
view of our past.

Yet many other tantalizing bits and pieces unearthed offer a
very different story of what really happened. Called "out-of-place
artifacts," they don't fit the "established" pattern of prehistory,
pointing back instead to the existence of advanced civilizations
before any of the known ancient cultures came into being.

Though such discoveries with their inherent sophistication
are well documented, most historians would like to sweep these
disturbing anomalies under the proverbial rug. But the "rug" of
true history is getting very lumpy, and hard to step across without tripping over such obvious contradictions to the conservative picture of antiquity.

What's more, the mysterious artifacts confirm ancient legends and stories which describe human history not as linear, but
cyclic. Forgotten ages and former worlds rose and fell in great
cycles of life and death over millions of years, lost to our memo-

Reprinted from Atlantis Rising Magazine, issue #4.

ry except in myths, and now, through a few amazing pieces left to us. Here are the "top ten" out-of-place artifacts and what they reveal to us about our missing legacy:

1. BAFFLING BATTERIES OF BABYLON

In 1938, Dr. Wilhelm Kong, an Austrian archaeologist rummaging through the basement of the museum made a find that was to drastically alter all concepts of ancient science. A 6-inch-high pot of bright yellow clay dating back two millennia contained a cylinder of sheet-copper 5 inches by 1.5 inches. The edge of the copper cylinder was soldered with a 60-40 lead-tin alloy comparable to today's best solder. The bottom of the cylinder was capped with a crimped-in copper disk and sealed with bitumen or asphalt.

Baghdad battery

Another insulating layer of asphalt sealed the top and also held in place an iron rod suspended into the center of the copper cylinder. The rod showed evidence of having been corroded with acid. With a background in mechanics, Dr. Konig recognized this configuration was not a chance arrangement, but that the clay pot was nothing less than an ancient electric battery.

The ancient battery in the Baghdad Museum as well as those others which were unearthed in Iraq all date from the Parthian Persian occupation between 248 B.C. and A.D. 226. However, Konig found copper vases plated with silver in the Baghdad Museum excavated from Sumerian remains in southern Iraq dating back to at least 2500 B.C. When the vases were lightly tapped a blue patina or film separated from the surfaces, characteristic of silver electroplated to copper. It would appear then that the Persians inherited their batteries from the earliest known civilization in the Middle East.

2. THE STRANGE ELECTRON TUBES FROM DENDERA

In different locations within the Late Ptolemaic Temple of Hathor at Dendera in Egypt are curious wall engravings which Egyptologists cannot explain in traditional religio-mythic terms, but about which electrical engineers are finding very modern interpretations.

In one chamber, No. 17, the topmost panel, depicts Egyptian priests operating what look like oblong tubes, performing various specific tasks. Each tube has a serpent extending its full length inside. Swedish engineer Henry Kjellson, in his book *Forvunen Teknik* (Disappeared Technology), noted that in the hieroglyphs these serpents are translated as seref, which means "to glow," and believes it refers to some form of electrical current. In the scene, to the extreme right appears a box on top where sits an image of the Egyptian god Atum-Ra, which identifies the box as the energy source. Attached to the box is a braided cable which electromagnetics engineer Alfred D. Bielek identified as virtually an exact copy of engineering illustrations used today for representing a bundle of conducting electrical wires. The cable runs from the box the full length of the floor of the picture, and terminates at both the ends and at the bases of the tube objects. These objects each rest on a pillar called a djed, which Bielek identified as a high-voltage insulator.

The tube objects look very much like TV picture tubes, an impression which is not far from wrong, for electronics technician N. Zecharius has identified the objects as Crookes or electron tubes, the forerunner of the modern television tube.

Though the upper chamber scenes have been damaged by vandals from a later age, other pictures found inside the "crypt" below the Holy of Holies are almost perfectly preserved, and their portrayal deepens the mystery of the strange electron tubes even further. Here, not only are the tubes shown in full operation, but something else has been added which may suggest the ultimate purpose for the tubes themselves. In several instances, both men and women are shown sitting underneath the tubes, hands held out and cupped, which meant they were in a receptive mode. What kind of "radiation treatment" was being performed here?

3. THE ENIGMA OF THE ASHOKA PILLAR

A testimony to ancient metallurgical skills in Delhi, India is called the Ashoka Pillar. Standing over 23 feet, it averages 16 inches in diameter and weighs about 6 tons. The solid wrought-iron shaft is made up of expertly welded discs. An inscription on the base is an epitaph to King Chandra Gupta II, who died in A.D. 413.

Despite being well over a millennium and a half in age, the Pillar's constitution is remarkably preserved. The smooth surface is like polished brass with only occasional instances of pock-marks and weathering. The mystery is that any equivalent mass of iron, subjected to the Indian monsoon rains, winds and temperatures for 1,600 years or more would have been reduced to rust long ago.

Production of the iron and the techniques of preservation are far beyond 5th century abilities. It is probably far older—maybe several thousand years. Who were the mysterious metallurgists who made this wonder, and what happened to their civilization?

Ashoka pillar

4. AN OUT-OF-PLACE COMPUTER FROM ANTIKYTHERA

A few days before Easter Sunday in 1900, Greek sponge divers off the small island of Antikythera discovered the remains of an ancient ship filled with bronze and marble statues and assorted artifacts later dated between 85 and 50 B.C. Among the finds was a small formless lump of corroded bronze and rotted wood, which was sent along with the other artifacts to the National Museum in Athens for further study. Soon, as the wood fragments dried and shrank from exposure to air, the lump split open revealing inside the outlines of a series of gear wheels like a modern clock.

In 1958 Dr. Derek J. de Solla Price successfully reconstructed the machine's appearance and use. The gearing system calculated the annual movements of the sun and moon. The arrangement shows that the gears could be moved forward and backward with ease at any speed. The device was thus not a clock but more like a calculator that could show the positions of the heavens past, present and future.

It is highly possible that the device may have origins ages long before the Greeks, and in a land far removed, now unknown.

5. FLIGHT IN ANCIENT EGYPT

In 1898 a curious winged object was discovered in the tomb of Pa-di-Imen in north Saqqara, Egypt dated to about 200 B.C. Because the birth of modern aviation was still several years away, when the strange artifact was sent to the Cairo Museum, it was

Saqqara glider

catalogued and then shelved among other miscellaneous items to gather dust.

Seventy years later, Dr. Kahlil Messiha—an Egyptologist and archaeologist—was examining a Museum display labeled "bird figurines." While most of the display were indeed bird sculptures, the Saqqara artifact was certainly not. It possessed characteristics never found on birds, yet which are part of modern aircraft design. Dr. Messiha, a former model plane enthusiast, immediately recognized the aircraft features and persuaded the Egyptian Ministry of Culture to investigate.

Made of very light sycamore the craft weighs 0.5 oz. with straight and aerodynamically shaped wings, spanning about 7 inches. A separate slotted piece fits onto the tail precisely like the back tail wing on a modern plane.

A full-scale version could have flown carrying heavy loads, but at low speeds, between 45 and 65 miles per hour. What is not known, however, is what the power source was. The model makes a perfect glider as it is. Even though over 2,000 years old, it will soar a considerable distance with only a slight jerk of the hand. Fully restored balsa replicas travel even farther.

Messiha notes that the ancient Egyptians often built scale models of everything familiar in their daily lives and placed them in their tombs—temples, ships, chariots, servants, animals and so forth. Now that we have found a model plane, Messiha wonders if perhaps somewhere under the desert sands there may yet be unearthed the remains of life-sized gliders.

6. A JET FROM SOUTH AMERICA

In 1954 the government of Colombia sent part of its collection of ancient gold artifacts on a U.S. tour. Emmanuel Staubs, one of America's leading jewelers, was commissioned to cast reproductions of six of the objects. Fifteen years later one was given to biologist-zoologist Ivan T. Sanderson for analysis. After a thorough examination and consulting a number of experts, Sanderson's mind-boggling conclusion was that the object is a model of a high-speed aircraft at least a thousand years old.

Approximately 2 inches long the object was worn as a pendant on a neck chain. It was classified as Sinu, a pre-Inca culture from A.D. 500 to 800. Both Sanderson and Dr. Arthur Poyslee of

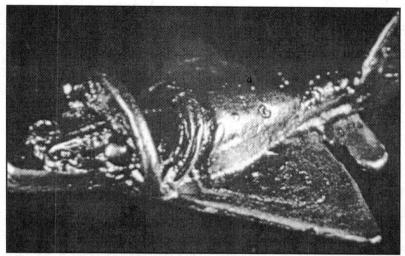

Columbia's golden jet

the Aeronautical Institute of New York concluded it did not represent any known winged animal. In fact, the little artifact appears more mechanical than biological. For example, the front wings are delta-shaped and rigidly straight edged, very un-animal-like.

The rudder is perhaps the most un-animal but airplane-like item. It is right-triangle, flat-surfaced, and rigidly perpendicular to the wings. Only fish have upright tail fins, but none have exclusively an upright flange without a counter-balancing lower one. Adding to the mystery, an insignia appears on the left face of the rudder—precisely where ID marks appear on many airplanes today. The insignia is perhaps as out-of place as the gold model itself, for it has been identified as the Aramaic or early Hebrew letter "beth" or B. This may indicate that the original plane did not come from Colombia, but was the product of a very early people inhabiting the Middle East who knew the secret of flying.

7. CRYSTAL SKULL FROM ATLANTIS?

Without doubt the most famous and enigmatic ancient crystal is the skull, discovered in 1927 by F.A. Mitchell-Hedges atop a ruined temple at the ancient Mayan city of Lubaantum, in British Honduras, now Belize.

The skull was made from a single block of clear quartz, 5 inches high, 7 inches long and 5 inches wide. It is about the size of a small human cranium, with near perfect detail. In 1970, art restorer Frank Dorland was given permission to submit the skull to tests at the Hewlitt-Packard Laboratories. Revealed were many anomalies.

The skull had been carved with total disregard to the natural crystal axis, a process unheard-of in modern crystallography. No metal tools were used. Dorland was unable to find any tell-tale scratch marks. Indeed, most metals would have been ineffectual. A modern penknife cannot mark it. From tiny patterns near the carved surfaces, Dorland determined it was first chiseled into rough form, probably using diamonds. The finer shaping, grinding and polishing, Dorland believes, was done with innumerable applications of water and silicon-crystal sand. If true, it would have taken 300 years of continuous labor. We must accept this almost unimaginable feat, or admit to the use of some form of lost technology.

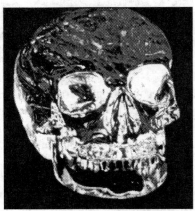

Crystal skull

Modern science is stumped to explain the skill and knowledge incorporated. As Garvin summarized: "It is virtually impossible today—in the time when men have climbed mountains on the moon—to duplicate this achievement....It would not be a question of skill, patience and time. It would simply be impossible. As one crystallographer from Hewlitt-Packard said, "The damned thing shouldn't be."

8. WHO SHOT NEANDERTHAL MAN?

The Museum of Natural History in London displays an early Paleolithic skull, dated at 38,000 years old, and excavated in 1921 in modern Zambia. On the left side of the skull is a perfectly round hole nearly a third of an inch in diameter. Curiously,

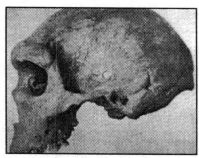

Neanderthal bullet hole

there are no radial split-lines around the hole or other marks that should have been left by a cold weapon, such as an arrow or spear. Opposite the hole, the cranium is shattered, and reconstruction of the fragments show the skull was blown from the inside out—as from a rifle shot. In fact, any slower a projectile would have produced neither the neat hole nor the shattering effect. Forensic experts who have examined the skull agree the cranial damage could not have been caused by anything but a high-speed projectile, purposely fired at the prehistoric victim, with intent to kill.

If such a weapon was indeed fired at the man, then one of two conclusions can be made: Either the specimen is not as old as it is claimed to be, and was shot by a European in recent centuries, or the remains are as old as claimed, and the marksman was ancient too. In view of the fact that the Paleolithic skull was excavated from a depth of 60 feet, mostly of lead rock, the second conclusion is more plausible. But who possessed gunpowder 38,000 years ago? Certainly not Stone Age man himself. Another race must have existed, one far more advanced and civilized, yet contemporary. The question is, where did that rifle-toting marksman call home?

9. THE INCREDIBLE STONES OF DR. CABRERA

A very unique time-capsule of images is housed in a warehouse in Ica, Peru. Here are some 20,000 stone boulders, tablets, and baseball-sized rocks, decorated with an astounding assortment of pictures, in many cases very much out of time and place. The owner is local physician, amateur archeologist and geologist Dr. Javier Cabrera

Ica brain surgery?

Darquea.

Most material employed is a gray andesite, an extremely hard granitic semi-crystalline matrix that is very difficult to carve. But as Dr. Cabrera observed, "People have been finding these engraved stones in the region for years." They were first seen and recorded by Jesuit missionary Father Simon, who accompanied Pizarro in 1525. Samples were shipped to Spain in 1562.

The stone portraits show very sophisticated surgery skills and medical knowledge—in some cases as advanced, and even more advanced, than today. There are scenes of Caesarean sections, blood transfusions, the use of acupuncture needles as an anesthetic (which only gained use in the West since the late 1970s), delicate operations on the lungs and kidneys, and removal of cancerous tumors. There are likewise detailed images of open heart and open brain surgery, as well as 20 stones showing a step-by-step heart transplant procedure.

This is a disturbing revelation in itself—that someone in unknown antiquity achieved a level of sophistication rivaling our own. But there are other pictures even more "out-of-place." As Dr. Cabrera noted, and as has been verified by other medical physicians, there are stone etchings which show a brain transplant. The prehistoric surgeons, it is evident, possessed knowledge several steps beyond modern-day surgery.

10. MANUFACTURED METALS MILLIONS OF YEARS OLD

For the past three decades miners at the Wonderstone Silver Mine near Ottosdal in the Western Transvaal, South Africa, have been extracting out of deep rock several strange metallic spheroids. So far at least 200 have been found. In 1979, several were closely examined by J.R. McIver, professor of geology at the University of Witwaterstand in Johannesburg, and geologist professor Andries Bisschoff of Potsshefstroom University.

The metallic spheroids look like flattened globes, averaging 1 to 4 inches in diam-

South African spheroid

eter, and their exteriors usually are colored steel blue with a reddish reflection, and embedded in the metal are tiny flecks of white fibers. They are made of a nickel-steel alloy which does not occur naturally, and is of a composition that rules them out, being of meteoric origin. Some have only a thin shell about a quarter of an inch thick, and when broken open are found filled with a strange spongy material that disintegrated into dust on contact with the air.

What makes all this very remarkable is that the spheroids were mined out of a layer of pyrophyllite rock, dated both geologically and by the various radio-isotope dating techniques as being at least 2.8 to 3 billion years old.

Adding mystery to mystery, Roelf Marx, curator of the South African Klerksdorp Museum, has discovered that the spheroid he has on exhibit slowly rotates on its axis by its own power, while locked in its display case and free of outside vibrations. There may thus be an energy extant within these spheroids still operating after three aeons of time.

2

Exposing a Scientific Coverup

by J. Douglas Kenyon

In 1966 respected archeologist Virginia Steen-McIntyre and her associates on a U.S. Geological Survey team working under a grant from the National Science Foundation were called upon to date a pair of remarkable archeological sites in Mexico. Sophisticated stone tools rivaling the best work of Cro-magnon man in Europe had been discovered at Hueyatlaco, while somewhat cruder implements had been turned up at nearby El Horno. The sites, it was conjectured, were very ancient, perhaps as old as 20,000 years, which, according to prevailing theories, would place them very close to the dawn of human habitation in the Americas.

Steen-McIntyre, knowing that if such antiquity could indeed be authenticated, her career would be made, set about an exhaustive series of tests. Using four different, but well accepted, dating methods, including uranium series and fission track, she determined to get it right. Nevertheless, when the results came in, the original estimates proved to be way off. Way *under*—as it turned out. The actual age was conclusively demonstrated to be more like a quarter of a million years.

As we might expect, some controversy ensued.

Steen-McIntyre's date challenged not only accepted chronologies for human presence in the region, but contradicted estab-

Reprinted from Atlantis Rising Magazine, issue #6.

lished notions of how long modern humans could have been anywhere on earth. Nevertheless, the massive reexamination of orthodox theory and the wholesale rewriting of textbooks which one might logically have expected did *not* ensue. What *did* follow was the public ridicule of Steen-McIntyre's work and the vilification of her character. She has not been able to find work in her field since.

More than a century earlier, following the discovery of gold in California's Table Mountain and the subsequent digging of thousands of feet of mining shafts, miners began to bring up hundreds of stone artifacts and even human fossils. Despite their origin in geological strata documented at 9 to 55 million years in age, California state geologist J. D. Whitney was able subsequently to authenticate many of the finds and to produce an extensive and authoritative report. The implications of Whitney's evidence have never been properly answered or explained by the establishment, yet the entire episode has been virtually ignored and references to it have vanished from the textbooks.

For decades miners in South Africa have been turning up— from strata nearly three billion years in age—hundreds of small metallic spheres with encircling parallel grooves. Thus far, the scientific community has failed to take note.

Among scores of such cases cited in the recently published *Forbidden Archeology* (and in the condensed version *The Hidden History of the Human Race*) it is clear that these three are by no means uncommon. Suggesting nothing less than a "massive coverup," co-authors Michael Cremo and Richard Thompson believe that when it comes to explaining the origins of the human race on earth, academic science has cooked the books.

While the public may believe that all the real evidence supports the mainstream theory of evolution—with its familiar timetable for human development (i.e., Homo Sapiens of the modern type going back to only about 100,000 years)—Cremo and Thompson demonstrate that, to the contrary, a virtual mountain of evidence produced by reputable scientists applying standards just as exacting, if not more so, than the establishment has been not only ignored but, in many cases, actually suppressed. In every area of research, from paleontology to anthropology and archeology, that which is presented to the public as established

Michael Cremo

and irrefutable fact is indeed nothing more, says Cremo, "than a consensus arrived at by powerful groups of people."

Is that consensus justified by the evidence? Cremo and Thompson say no.

Carefully citing all available documentation, the authors produce case after case of contradictory research conducted in the last two centuries. Included are detailed descriptions of the controversy and ultimate suppression following each discovery. Typical is the case of George Carter who claimed to have found, at an excavation in San Diego, hearths and crude stone tools at levels corresponding to the last interglacial period, some 80,000-90,000 years ago. Even though Carter's work was endorsed by some experts such as lithic scholar John Witthoft, the establishment scoffed. San Diego State University refused to even look at the evidence in its own back yard and Harvard University publicly defamed him in a course on "Fantastic Archeology."

What emerges is a picture of an arrogant and bigoted academic elite interested more in the preservation of its own prerogatives and authority than the truth.

Illinois "Coin" found at a depth of 114 feet in glacial deposits

Needless to say, the weighty (952 page) volume has caused more than a little stir. The establishment, as one might expect, is outraged, albeit having a difficult time ignoring the book. Anthropologist Richard Leakey wrote, "Your book is pure humbug and does not deserve to be taken seriously by anyone but a fool." Nevertheless, many prestigious scientific publications including *The American Journal of Physical Anthropology, Geo Archeology*, and the British *Journal for the History of Science* have deigned to review the book, and while generally critical of its arguments, have conceded, though grudgingly, that *Forbidden Archeology* is well written and well researched. Some indeed recognize a significant challenge to the prevailing theories. As William Howells wrote in *Physical Anthropologist*, "To have modern human beings...appearing a great deal earlier, in fact at a time when even simple primates did not exist as possible ancestors, would be devastating not only to the accepted pattern, it would be devastating to the whole theory of evolution, which has been pretty robust up until now."

Yet despite its considerable challenge to the evolutionary edifice, *Forbidden Archeology* chooses not to align itself with the familiar creationist point of view nor to attempt an alternative theory of its own. The task of presenting his own complex theory—which seeks, he says, to avoid the "false choice," usually presented in the media between evolution and creationism—Cremo has reserved as the subject of a forthcoming book *Human Evolution*. On the question of human origins, he insists, "we really do have to go back to the drawing board."

As the author told *Atlantis Rising* recently, "*Forbidden Archaeology* suggests the real need for an alternative explanation, a new synthesis. I'm going to get into that in detail. And it's going to have elements of the Darwinian idea, and elements of the ancient astronaut theory, and elements of the creationist nature, but it's going to be much more complex. I think we've become accustomed to overly simplistic pictures of human origins, whereas the reality is a little more complicated than any advocates of the current ideas are prepared to admit."

Both Cremo and Thompson are members of the Bhaktivedanta Institute—the Science Studies Branch of the International Society for Krishna consciousness. Cremo and Thompson started their project with the goal of finding evidence to corroborate the ancient Sanskrit writings of India which relate episodes of human history going back millions of years.

"So we thought," says Cremo, "if there's any truth to those ancient writings, there should be some physical evidence to back it up but we really didn't find it in the current textbooks." They didn't stop there though. Over the next eight years Cremo and Thompson investigated the entire history of archeology and anthropology, delving into everything that has been discovered, not just what has been reported in textbooks. What they found was a revelation. "I thought there might be a few little things that have been swept under the rug," said Cremo, "but what I found was truly amazing. There's actually a massive amount of evidence that's been suppressed."

Cremo and Thompson determined to produce a book of irrefutable archeological facts. "The standard used," says Cremo, "(meant) the site had to be identifiable, there had to be good geological evidence on the age of the site and there had to be some reporting about it, in most cases in the scientific literature." The

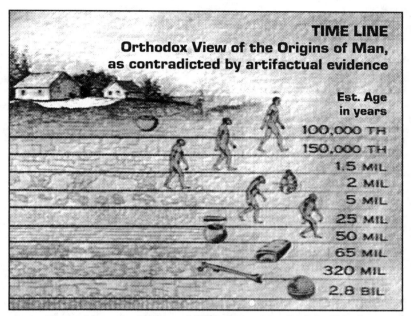

TIME LINE
Orthodox View of the Origins of Man,
as contradicted by artifactual evidence

Est. Age
in years

100,000 TH
150,000 TH
1.5 MIL
2 MIL
5 MIL
25 MIL
50 MIL
65 MIL
320 MIL
2.8 BIL

Revised from the NBC special "The Mysterious Origins of Man"

quality and quantity of the evidence—they hoped—would compel serious examination by professionals in the field, as well as by students and the general public.

Few would deny that they have succeeded in spectacular fashion. Much in demand in alternative science circles, the authors have also found a sympathetic audience among the self-termed sociologists of scientific knowledge, who are very aware of the failure of modern scientific method to present a truly objective picture of reality. An upcoming NBC special, "The Mysterious Origins of Man" draws heavily upon Cremo and Thompson's suggestion that there is a "knowledge filter" among the scientific elite which has given us a picture of prehistory which is largely incorrect.

The problem, Cremo believes, is both misfeasance and malfeasance. "You can find many cases where it's just an automatic process. It's just human nature that a person will tend to reject things that don't fit in with his particular world view." He cites the example of a young paleontologist and expert on ancient whale bones at the Museum of Natural History in San Diego.

When asked if he ever saw signs of human marks on any of the bones, the scientist remarked, "I tend to stay away from anything that has to do with humans because it's just too controversial." Cremo sees the response as an innocent one from someone interested in protecting his career. In other areas, though, he perceives something much more vicious, as in the case of Virginia Steen-McIntyre. "What she found was that she wasn't able to get her report published. She lost the teaching position at the university. She was labeled a publicity seeker and a maverick in her profession. And she really hasn't been able to work as a professional geologist since then."

In other examples, Cremo finds even broader signs of deliberate malfeasance. He mentions the activities of the Rockefeller foundation, which funded Davidson Black's research at Zhoukoudian (in China). Correspondence between Black and his superiors with the Foundation shows that research and archeology was part of a far larger biological research project, (from the correspondence) "thus we may gain information about our behavior of the sort that can lead to wide and beneficial control." In other words, this research was being funded with the specific goal of control. "Control by whom?" Cremo wants to know.

The motive to manipulate is not so hard to understand. "There's a lot of social power connected with explaining who we are and what we are," he says. "Somebody once said 'knowledge is power.' You could also say power is knowledge. Some people have particular power and prestige that enables them to dictate the agenda of our society. I think it's not surprising that they are resistant to any change."

Cremo agrees that scientists today have become a virtual priest class, exercising many of the rights and prerogatives which their forebears in the industrial scientific revolution sought to wrest from an entrenched religious establishment. "They set the tone and the direction for our civilization on a worldwide basis," he says. "If you want to know something today you usually don't go to a priest or a spiritually inclined person, you go to one of these people because they've convinced us that our world is a very mechanistic place, and everything can be explained mechanically by the laws of physics and chemistry which are currently accepted by the establishment."

To Cremo it seems the scientists have usurped the keys of the kingdom, and then failed to live up to their promises. "In many ways the environmental crisis and the political crisis and the crisis in values is their doing. And I think many people are becoming aware that (the scientists) really haven't been able to deliver the kingdom to which they claimed to have the keys. I think many people are starting to see that the world view they are presenting just doesn't account for everything in human experience."

For Cremo we are all part of a cosmic hierarchy of beings, a view for which he finds corroboration in world mythologies. "If you look at all of those traditions, when they talk about origins they don't talk about it as something that just occurs on this planet. There are extraterrestrial contacts with gods, demigods, goddesses, angels." And he feels there may be parallels in the modern UFO phenomenon.

The failure of modern science to satisfactorily deal with UFOs, extra-sensory perception or the paranormal provides one of the principal charges against it. "I would have to say that the evidence of such today is very strong," he argues. "It's very difficult to ignore. It's not something that you can just sweep away. If you were to just reject all of the evidence for UFOs, abductions and other kinds of contacts coming from so many reputable sources, it seems we have to give up accepting any kind of human testimony whatsoever."

One area where orthodoxy has been frequently challenged is in the notion of sudden change brought about by enormous cataclysm, versus the gradualism usually conceived of by evolutionists. Even though it has become fashionable to talk of such events, they have been relegated to the very distant past supposedly before the appearance of man. Yet some like Immanual Velikovsky and others have argued that many such events have occurred in our past and induced a kind of planetary amnesia from which we still suffer today.

That such catastrophic episodes have occurred and that humanity has suffered from some great forgettings, Cremo agrees. "I think there is a kind of amnesia which when we encounter the actual records of catastrophes, it makes us think, oh well, this is just mythology. In other words, I think some knowledge of these catastrophes does survive in ancient writings and cultures and through oral traditions. But because of what you might call some social amnesia, as we encounter those things we are not able to accept them as truth. I also think there's a deliberate attempt on the part of those who are now in control of the world's intellectual life to make us disbelieve and forget the paranormal and related phenomena. I think there's a definite attempt to keep us in a state of forgetfulness about these things."

It's all part of the politics of ideas. Says Cremo, "It's been a struggle that's been going on thousands and thousands of years and it's still going on."

"Electron Tubes" in operation from Egyptian Temple of Dendura? (courtesy of Joseph Jochmans)

The Great Pyramid of Giza

The Temple at Luxor

Dr. Virginia Steen-McIntyre as seen on NBC's "Mysterious Origins of Man"

Robert Bauval, author of "The Orion Mystery"

John Anthony West on NBC's Emmy winning "The Mystery of the Sphinx"

"Fingerprints of the Gods" author Graham Hancock on a BBC special

The "Bent" pyramid of Dahshur

Mohenjo Daro

Candi Sukah in Central Java

The Sphinx (cover photograph for issue #1 of "Atlantis Rising")

The Wall at Edfu

Sophisticated art from ancient cave dwellers at Lascaux, France

Athanasius Kircher's 1665 map of Atlantis

Poseidon the "god" of Atlantis

Artist Tom Miller's conjecture of what archeology in Antarctica
might be like (cover art for issue #7 of "Atlantis Rising")

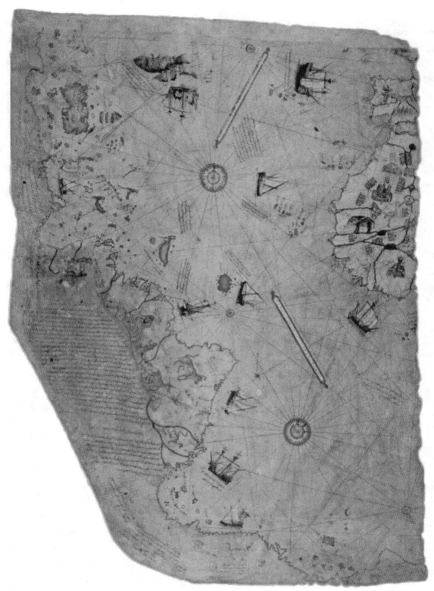

The 1513 Piri Ri'is map of the Atlantic

A diver examines the "J road" near Bimini in the Bahamas.

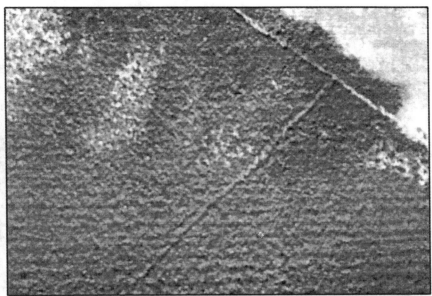
Prehistoric channels connecting 12 artesian wells on island of North Bimini.

Semi-circular arrangement of prehistoric stones beneath waters near Bimini

"The Destruction of Atlantis" painted by Tom Miller

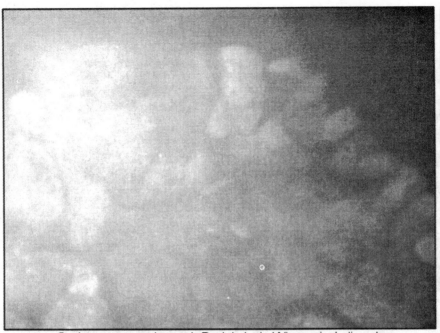

Sunken structure beneath Rock Lake in Wisconsin, believed
by archeologist Frank Joseph to be Atlantean ruins
(photo from "The Ancient American")

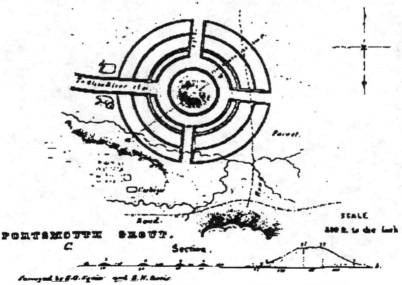

A survey of excavations near Portsmouth, Ohio, as published
by the Smithsonian Museum in their first book "Ancient
Monuments of the Mississippi Valley" (1848) which archeologist
Jackson Judge says exactly mirrors Plato's Atlantis.

Overview of Kalasaya Temple at Tiahuanaco, Peru. NBC's special "The Mysterious Origins of Man," using astronomical calculations, documented the temple's age at 16,900 B.C. (Photo by Carol Cote)

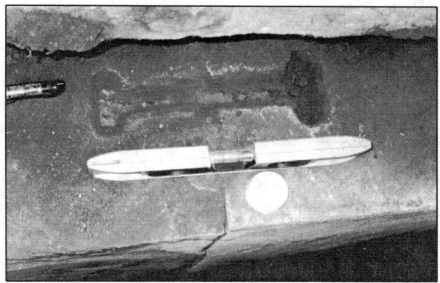

Location of a bronze clamp used to join two massive blocks in the Kalasaya Temple. Advanced technology is indicated by evidence that bronze was poured into the slot from some kind of portable smelter.
(Photo by Carol Cote)

Zecharia Sitchin next to the statue of the Pharoah Amenhotep II, whom he believes to be the Pharoah of the Exodus.

Sitchin believes this ancient Sumerian City doubled as a spaceport

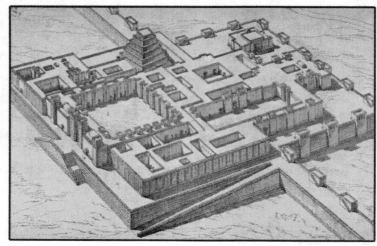

Space researcher Richard Hoagland

Artist Tom Miller's conjecture
of what ancient ruins on the
moon might look like up close
(Cover art for "Atlantis Rising"
Issue #2)

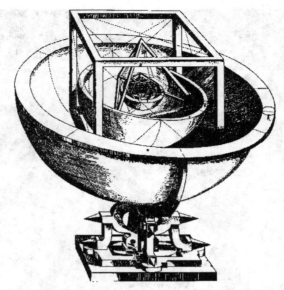

Is the Earth only a crystalline structure evolving in a larger cosmic crystal grid? Kepler saw the orbits of the planets as defined by Platonic forms.

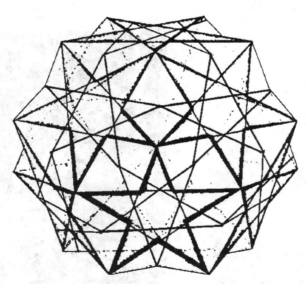

The apostle John's vision of the New Jerusalem in Revalations Chapter 21 —the double penta-dodecahedron crystal form, composed of twelve double pentacles based on the golden mena proportion.

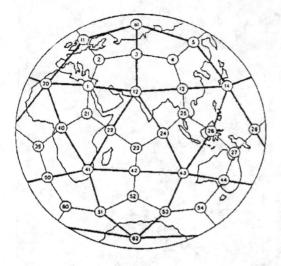

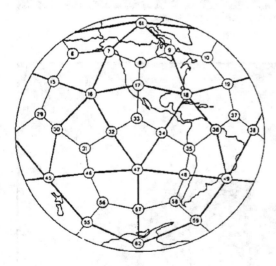

A SAMPLING OF MONUMENTS FOUND AT MAJOR NODE POINTS ALONG THE CRYSTAL GRID

1. Great Pyramid, Egypt

4. Shamballa, Gobi Desert, Outer Mongolia

5. Yakut pyramid structure, Siberia

8. Medicine Wheel concentration, Canada

9. Inukshuk cairns, North Magnetic Pole

11. Callanish stone circle, Scotland

12. Mohenjo Daro ruins, Pakistan

13. Shensi Pyramids, China

14. Deep submerged ruins, Devil's Sea, off Japan

16. Sacred platforms, Hawaii

17. Four Corners kivas, American Southwest

18. Sunken ruins off Bimini, Bahamas

20. Megalithic complex, Algeria

21. Angiarro sphinx, mounds, Ethiopia

25. Anghkor Wat temple complex, Cambodia

26. Megaliths, Borneo

28. Nan Madol stone city, Pohnpei, Caroline Is.

31. Maiden complex; Tongareva stone circles

32. Nuku Hiva ruins, Marquesas Is.

35. Cuzco/Machu Picchu sacred centers, Peru

36. Paramaribo inscribed blocks, Surinam

41. Great Zimbabwe ruins, Zimbabwe

44. Koonunda stone circle, Australia

45. Paita cylinders, New Caledonia

46. Rimatara stone columns, Tabuai Is.

47. Rapa Nui stone heads, Easter Island

49. Gavea stone sphinx, Rio de Janiero, Brazil

61. Hyperborean remains, North Pole, Arctic

62. Polarian remains, South Pole, Antarctica

Artist Tom Miller speculates about Earth's crystal grid

Were megalithic sites such as Stonehenge tuned to an Earth grid?

Do the sands of the Sahara conceal the wreakage of a lost civilization?

Is Atlantis buried under thousands of feet of ice in Antarctica?

Do native American ruins such as these at Mesa Verde National Park
contain clues to coming Earth changes?

Temple of the Sun, Mesa Verde

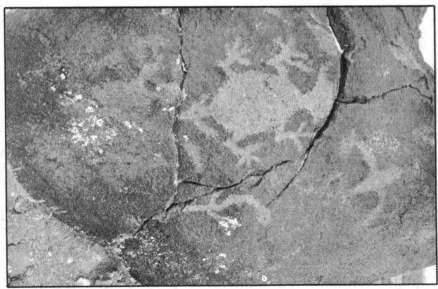
Petroglyph, Mesa Verde

In "Atlantis Rising Magazine's" serialized graphic novel "The Atlantis Dimension," the lives of several individuals are followed from ancient Atlantis to modern times, where they encounter the consequences of actions taken millennia ago. Sumara, a temple priestess and her lover Ramnon reincarnate in contemporary Miami as Kristine and Keith, an artist and a network reporter. Keith is unexpectedly diverted from pursuing his nemesis, a major drug lord known as "Saturn," to an underwater search for Atlantis in the Bahamas led by archeologist Bjorn Leyerdorf, Kristine's father. The ultimate discovery of the long-sought ruins leads to a confrontation with Saturn and a revisiting of the origins of current events in ancient Atlantis.

the Atlantis Dimension

Written by J. Douglas Kenyon
and N. Thomas Miller
Illustrated by Rob Rath

The Callanish Stones of the Isle of Lewis, part of a connection between the British Isles and Atlantis?

Is the foundation of Jerusalem's Western Wall, a gigantic stone from Atlantis?

No one knows when Machu Picchu was built high on a jungle mountain top in Peru but almost certainly it was long before the Incas.

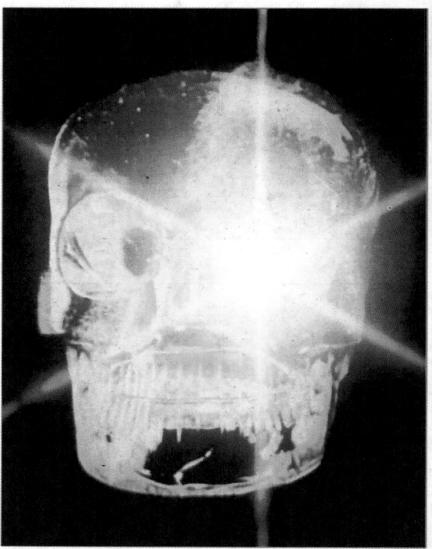

Prismatic effect caused by laser light projected into the Mitchell-Hedges Crystal Skull (courtesy of Joseph Jochmans).

3

Evolution? Creation? Or Is There More to the Story?

by David Lewis

Genesis, the Biblical story of creation, tells us God created the universe in six days. He made Adam, the first man, the Bible tells us, from the dust of the earth, an event many Christians believe took place in the Garden of Eden 6,000 years ago. Scientists and religious scholars call this scenario creationism. In 1859, Charles Darwin came up with another idea. He said man's existence could be explained within the context of material creation alone, through evolution and natural selection, the survival of the fittest. According to Darwin, man evolved from apes, an idea distinctly at odds with the Biblical scenario.

The debate over human origins has raged ever since. It surfaced more recently in Abbotsford, British Columbia, where a school board dominated by Christians requires the teaching of *Intelligent Design*, a form of creationism, along with the theory of evolution. Reports Maclean's Magazine, "The issue they are debating is a large one ... arguably the biggest question of them all: how did life begin ... with a Big Bang or a Big Being?"

Critics of the Abbotsford policy fear the school board would place the Book of Genesis on a par with Darwin's Origin of Species. They accuse the board of imposing their religious beliefs on students, while some Christians believe that teaching Darwinism amounts to the same thing, the imposition of a *de facto* religious

Reprinted from Atlantis Rising Magazine, issue #6.

belief system.

Recent studies show, however, that adherents to either side of this wrangle would do well to rethink their positions. A reexamination of old and new research reveals that the creationism versus Darwinism debate may be missing the mark entirely.

Richard Thompson and Michael Cremo, co-authors of *Forbidden Archeology* and *The Hidden History of the Human Race*, have assembled a body of evidence that testifies to the existence of modern man millions of years before his supposed emergence from southern Africa 100,000 years ago. On *The Mysterious Origins of Man*, an NBC documentary which first aired in February of 1996, Thompson and Cremo make their case along with other experts. The evidence they reveal suggests man neither evolved from apes nor rose from the dust of the earth just 4,000 years before the time of Christ. The implications are profound and may force a reevaluation of the entire issue of human origins.

Narrated by Charlton Heston and drawing on evidence largely ignored by the scientific establishment, *Mysterious Origins* steps outside the usual Bible versus Darwin debate. At issue are human footprints discovered in Texas side by side with dinosaur tracks, stone tools dating back 55 million years, sophisticated maps of unknown antiquity, and evidence of advanced civilization in prehistory.

Darwin lampooned in an
1871 cartoon

Based on research assembled as Darwin began to dominate scientific thought at the turn of the century, and upon more recent archaeological discoveries, *Mysterious Origins* exposes a "knowledge filter" within the scientific establishment, a bias that favors accepted dogma while rejecting evidence that does not support conventional theory. As a result, fossil evidence indicating man is far more ancient than conventional theory allows, and that he did not evolve from apes, has gathered dust for over a century, suppressed, in effect, because it conflicts with an entrenched belief system, the NBC documentary reveals. Scientists, moreover, who challenge accepted dogma, can find themselves not only on the outside of the debate, but unemployed.

Thompson, science investigator Richard Milton, and other experts trace the problem to "speculative leaps" made by researchers too eager to find the missing link in human evolution, the long-sought-after ancestor of both man and apes. "It seems any missing link will do," Milton says, regarding the 120-year effort to prove Darwin's theory.

In the case of so-called Pithecanthropus Ape man (a.k.a. Java Man, *homo erectus*), anthropologist Eugene Dubois found a human thigh bone and the skull cap of an ape, in Indonesia, separated by a distance of forty feet. The year was 1891. He pieced the two together, creating the famous Java Man. But many experts say the thigh bone and skull cap are unrelated. Shortly before his death, Dubois himself said the skull cap belonged to a large monkey, and the thigh bone to a man. Yet Java Man remains to this day, to many, evidence of man's descent from apes, having been featured in New York's Museum of Natural History until 1984.

In the case of *Piltdown Man*, another missing link wanna-be found in England in 1910, the find proved to be a sophisticated fraud perpetrated, in all likelihood, by overly zealous Darwinists. And even the crown jewel of alleged human ancestral fossils, the famous *Lucy*, found in Ethiopia in 1974, is indistinguishable from a monkey or extinct ape, according to many anthropologists.

Physical anthropologist Charles Oxnard, and other scientists, have drawn a picture of human evolution radically at odds with the conventional theory, a fact usually ignored by universities and natural history museums. Oxnard placed the genus Homo, to which man belongs, in a far more ancient time period than standard evolutionary theory allows, bringing into question the underpinnings of Darwin's theory. As reported in Cremo and Thompson's *Hidden History*, Oxnard states, "The conventional notion of human evolution must now be heavily modified or even rejected ... new concepts must be explored."

What pains other opponents of standard evolutionary theory is its inability to account for how new species and features originate, the supposition that the innumerable aspects of biological life, down to the pores in human skin, a beetle's legs, the protective pads on a camel knees, and on and on, came about accidentally through natural selection. The notion of intent, or inherent purpose, within creation does not fit into the Darwinian version of reality. Life, to a Darwinist, can only exist in the context of absolute materialism, a series of accidental events and chemical reactions responsible for everything in the universe. Even common sense seems to take a back seat to scientific dogma. In the case of the human brain, for instance, its advanced capacities (the ability to perform calculus, play the violin, consciousness itself) cannot be explained by the survival of the fittest doctrine alone.

What about the Bible and Creationism?

The creationist argument derives from orthodox religious doctrine, rejecting allegorical and metaphorical interpretations of the Book of Genesis. It is a belief system many Christians do not accept literally and which the Bible itself may not support. It also lacks scientific support, in that fossil records reveal man has existed on earth for far longer than 6,000 years. The six days of creation scenario, moreover, taken literally, bears no resemblance to the time it took for the universe to be born. The more common-sense notion of *Intelligent Design*, however, creationism without the dogma, strikes a more palatable note, even among some scientists, who find it hard to deny that an inherent intelligence exists within the universe. The problem with creationism lies, then, not in the idea of intelligent design, but in dogmatic interpretations of the Bible, the lack of mental flexibility shared by both extremes in the debate over human origins.

New Ground or Ancient Wisdom?

Evidence for extremely ancient human origins will lead many into foreign territory, terrain some would rather avoid. But to others, the standard creationism versus evolution debate was wanting all along. Once looked upon with raised eyebrows, and still facing dogged opposition, the *catastrophist* point of view has made headway of late in the scientific community. This theory says that sudden disruptions in the continuity of planetary life have taken place, altering the course of evolution (Gradualism, on the other hand, a Darwinist tenet that assumes all life evolved slowly and without interruption, has fallen out of favor in some circles). Indeed, it has become clear that all sorts of catastrophes have taken place on the globe, and in the universe at large. A well-known catastrophist theory proposes that the extinction of the dinosaurs resulted from a huge meteor crashing into the planet with the force of thousands of hydrogen bombs. Other theories have to do with drastic changes in climate, seismic upheavals and fluctuations, even reversals, in the earth's magnetic field.

The catastrophism versus gradualism debate, while revealing how little science knows for certain about prehistory, also exposes a distinct prejudice within the scientific community—an antipathy, dating to the time of Darwin, toward anything remotely resembling Biblical catastrophes, such as the great flood, even if the connection has only to do with sudden, rather than gradual, changes in the course of evolution.

Catastrophism, though, avails another scenario regarding human origins and prehistory. As presented in Graham Hancock's *Fingerprints of the Gods* and in Rand and Rose Flem-Ath's *When the Sky Fell*, a sudden, catastrophic shifting of the earth's lithosphere, called crustal displacement, may have occurred at some time in the past. Lent credibility by Albert Einstein, the theory suggests that the earth's outer crust may have suddenly (not gradually, as in *Continental Drift*) shifted on the surface of the globe, causing continents to slide into radically different positions.

Drawing on the work of Charles Hapgood, who developed the theory with Einstein's assistance, the Flem-Aths explain that this may be the reason carcasses of hundreds of woolly mammoths, rhinos and other ancient mammals were found flash-frozen in a "zone of death" across Siberia and northern Canada. Remarkably, the stomachs of these mammals contained warm-weather plants, the implication being that the very ground upon which the animals grazed suddenly shifted from a temperate to an Arctic climate. Hapgood and Einstein theorized that a sudden shifting and freezing of the continent of Antarctica, which may have been situated 2,000 miles farther north than it is now, may have occurred as a result of crustal displacement.

Ancient maps, accurately depicting Antarctica before it was covered in ice, also support the idea that the continent was situated in a temperate climate in recent prehistory. Copied from source maps of unknown antiquity, the Piri Reis, Oronteus Finaeus and Mercator maps derive, Graham Hancock and the Flem-Aths propose, from some prehistoric society with the capacity to accurately calculate longitude and chart coastlines, an accomplishment that did not take place in recorded history until the eighteenth century. As outlined in Flem-Ath and Hancock's books, the maps, along with a body of evidence, testify to the existence of a sophisticated prehistoric civilization. Charlton Heston, on NBC's *Mysterious Origins*, likens this scenario to Plato's description of the lost continent of Atlantis.

Lost Civilizations, the real missing link?

Examining stone work at ancient cites in Bolivia, Peru, and Egypt, Hancock argues that these megalithic marvels could not have risen from the dust of nomadic hunter-gatherers, which is what conventional science would have us believe. The magnificent city of Tiahuanaco, Bolivia, emerges as a case in point, said by Bolivian scholar, Arthur Poznansky, to date to 15,000 B.C. Precision stone cuttings performed on immense blocks at Tiahuanaco, and at the other cites, to tolerances of one-fiftieth of an inch, and then the transporting of these blocks over long distances, reveal technical capacities that match or surpass those of modern engineers. How supposedly primitive people transported these megaliths, to the summit of Machu Picchu in Peru, for instance, remains a great mystery, feats that conventional scientific theories are at a loss to explain. Hancock asserts that, even if we accept the later dates most archaeologists ascribed to these structures, the knowledge and technical abilities of the builders would had to have been the product of a civilization that evolved over a long period of time, pushing the appearance of civilized man to the predawn of recorded history.

"My view," Hancock says, "is that we are looking at a common influence that touched all of these places, long before recorded history, a remote third-party civilization yet to be identified by historians."

A wide range of natural evidence and recorded human experience points to the existence of such a civilization. Etymology, the study of word origins, postulates that a prehistoric Indo-European language must have existed to account for the deep similarities in the world's languages. Could this have been the language of Hancock's prehistoric civilization?

Santillana's *Hamlet's Mill*, a study of how ancient myths depict the precession of the equinoxes, weighs in also, testifying to the existence of advanced knowledge proliferated among prehistoric peoples. Discussing myths that originate in the mists of antiquity, and the numerical values and symbology recorded therein, Santillana reveals that the ancients of many cultures shared a sophisticated knowledge of celestial mechanics that has only recently been matched with the help of satellites and computers. The proliferation of closely related biological species on continents separated by vast oceans, a phenomenon that puzzles Darwinists, can also be explained by the existence of an advanced, seafaring civilization in prehistory. An entire body of evidence, in fact, supports man and civilization having existed at a far earlier date than orthodox science or religion concedes. Could the existence, then, of such a civilization, be the *real* missing link in human history?

Why limit the debate to Western models?

The conventional debate over our origins, as we find it characterized in the major media, ignores concepts of human and cosmic origins shared by a large portion of the world's population, those of the mystic East. Einstein himself entertained such ideas, because they supported his belief in a universal intelligence. More recently, physicist and Nobel Laureate Brian Josephson, and others, have drawn parallels between Eastern mysticism and modern physics. Fritjof Capra, in *The Tao of Physics*, harmonizes Vedic, Buddhist and Taoist philosophy with the subtleties of quantum theory. The Vedas, in fact, present a scenario similar to the expanding and contracting universe of modern physics, the Great In breath and Out breath of creation, the projection of omnipresent consciousness, Brahman, the essence of

Albert Einstein with Hindu Holy Man

which remains intrinsic to all things as creation evolves. Taoism, on the other hand, offers an understanding of conscious reality that closely resembles Heisenberg's *uncertainty principle*, where perspective, or consciousness, shapes objective reality.

To Einstein, especially in his later years, the idea of consciousness-based reality became naturally apparent, as it does now to others in the field of physics, philosophy, and religion, the awareness of a universal, conscious presence inseparable from identity and creation. "As I grow older," Einstein said," the identification with the here and now [his famous space-time] is slowly lost. One feels dissolved, merged into nature."

The greatest minds, then, of our time and of the greatest antiquity reject Darwin's often unstated premise, his belief in absolute materialism, which says that all life evolved from primitive matter, accidentally, without purpose or design. At the same time, consciousness-based creation offers an alternative to strict Biblical interpretations and the concept of an anthropomorphic creator separate from man and nature.

Establishment science, though, has had a hands-off approach to consciousness, never daring to explore what by definition cannot be explained by matter-based beliefs about the origin of life. An article in the December issue of Scientific American, by David Chalmers, *The Puzzle of Conscious Experience*, emphasizes the point.

"For many years," Chalmers says, "consciousness was shunned by researchers....The prevailing view was that science, which depends on objectivity, could not accommodate something as subjective as consciousness." Chalmers goes on to say that neuroscientists, psychologists and philosophers are only recently beginning to reject the idea that consciousness cannot be studied. He proposes, while insisting that consciousness is materially based, that "[it] might be explained by a new kind of theory ...[that] will probably involve new fundamental laws [with] startling consequences for our view of the universe and of ourselves."

The eminent physicist Steven Weinberg in his book *Dream of a Final Theory* puts it another way. He says the goal of physics is to develop a "theory of everything" that will tell us all there is to know about the universe—a law or principle from which the universe derives. So stating, Weinberg exposes the limitation of scientific materialism, while at the same time trying to transcend it, as he butts up against an Absolute, a Logos, if you will, that cannot exist within the context of matter-based creation. The real problem, he admits, is consciousness, because it is beyond what could have derived from material processes alone.

Darwinism, therefore, which depends upon the assumption that all existence is matter-based, cannot account for the most human characteristic of all, consciousness, which cannot derive from the process of natural selection in a random, mechanistic creation—the capacity of the human mind being far beyond what is necessary for mere survival. And strict creationism, when pitted against a Darwinism that ignores the origin of consciousness, along with other crucial factors, appears to be merely a foil that Darwinists use to make themselves look good.

To understand human origins, then, and to develop a *Theory of Everything*, a true scientist must not only evaluate the tangible evidence presented in *Forbidden Archeology*, and in *Finger-*

prints of the Gods, he must study consciousness, without which he neglects the most basic capacity of human beings—the ability to think creatively. He would have to experiment in the internal, subjective world, delving into what the scientific establishment considers a forbidden realm. He would have to devote himself, independent of any dogma, to the essence of his own conscious existence, as well as to the study of material creation. Like Einstein, he would see this pursuit as the essential goal of both science and religion, the search for knowledge in its purest sense, or *sciere* in the Latin, from which the word science derives. By so doing, science might arrive at a theory of everything.

PART TWO
THE EGYPTIAN CONNECTION

4

The Legacy de Lubicz
by Dr. Joseph Ray, Ph.D.

In *Serpent in the Sky: the High Wisdom of Ancient Egypt,* a well-written, scholarly and intellectually exciting work by John Anthony West, the intent is to make clear to a broad audience the remarkably fastidious and deeply insightful, if somewhat tedious, Egyptological research work of R. A. Schwaller de Lubicz, his family and a few colleagues That work began when R. A. went for vacation to Egypt with his wife Isha and stepdaughter Lucie Lamy. For 15 years they were immersed in and by it—returning then to Europe to ponder, organize and write. Lucie's *Egyptian Mysteries,* Isha's own extraordinary works and R. A.'s many treatises have all been published since. Thus the knowledge possessed by and, most significantly, the mode of thought engaged in by the highly elevated individuals who assembled, integrated and "embedded" that knowledge into hieroglyphs—as well as Pharaonic edifices, sculptures and paintings—continued to occupy most of their waking hours until the deaths of both R. A. and Isha. Lucie's *Egyptian Mysteries* was first published in 1981, by which time all the books by Isha and R. A. had appeared in print, in French. English readers are indebted to various translators who have, over the last 25 years, made available every one of them.

Serpent in the Sky is a great contribution to any thinking

Reprinted from Atlantis Rising Magazine, issue #1.

person's experience, but it's not "easy reading." How could it be? The subject matter is nothing less than a description, with examples par excellence, of a mode of thinking long totally foreign to us. So, we need to go slowly, to permit digestion. But, if we do, assimilation will take place, and months later, we'll notice subtle differences in our perceptions and understanding.

West helps us too. Throughout *Serpent...* in the wide margins are notes and quotations to illustrate the narrow mindedness and arrogance of the Egyptological establishment. Indeed, these "scholars" were so shaken by the painstaking work of Schwaller and his group that they ignored them—preferring the old "ostrich-head in the sand trick" or, as Jimmy Durante used to say, "my head's made up, don't confuse me with the facts." The tactic, though neither scholarly nor scientific, remains a favorite among such academics. Actually, it demonstrates a chief characteristic of what the ancient Egyptians called cerebral intelligence, the intelligence of the brain and the lower of the two intelligences potentially operative in us humans.

Schwaller's insights and conclusions that the ancient Egyptians thoroughly understood human psychology, physiology, anatomy as well as the mechanisms of genesis, the nature of numbers, the use and nature of forces and the human experience following bodily death were just too much to see, much less swallow. Easier to ignore it. The history of all areas of science is replete with similar stories, for despite contrary statements, scientific establishments function as do other bureaucracies. Individuals in the higher echelons do not happily receive ideas that contradict whatever they themselves have come to embrace and "feel comfortable with." Bureaucracies resist change but not for good reason.

In her *Opening of the Way, a Practical Guide to the Wisdom of Egypt,* Isha shows us that the ancient Egyptians understood why this is so. She characterizes cerebral intelligence and clarifies the organization and characteristics of brain consciousness and real consciousness as understood by these ancients. The personality, they said, is associated with brain consciousness and existed according to its values. These included: concern for the mundane, an orientation toward mediocrity, temporary (i.e. relative) values, emphasis on job-oriented education (!), temporality, superficiality and satisfaction. Real consciousness, associated with the intelligence-of-the-heart (that has its place in the brain), embraced different values, permanent, non-egoistic values along with an unequivocal, enduring love of life and of reality. Westerners, and Americans particularly, might find these ancient teachings disturbing, perhaps abhorrent. But such is the power of cerebral intelligence whose transcendence has brought about the life exterior superficial and unreal to an unprecedented degree.

These books suggest that the entirety of ancient Egyptian thought was ultimately directed to the possibility of and the means to accomplish a personal evolution. This was every human's purpose. The structures, edifices, paintings, sculptures and writings left in the temples and tombs were meant as examples of and teaching instruments for those who wished for the truth as then understood, to discover and put to use in their own lives. Repeatedly, Schwaller teaches that "everything is consciousness," that consciousness evolves in humanity only through individual effort.

Temple at Luxor

The architecture of the ancient Egyptian temples is itself sacred, incorporating profound wisdom and embodying the laws of nature that we "play" with today but have not understood. One might think we understood gravity, magnetism, electromagnetism, electricity, and life. In his *The Temple in Man* (published early in 1949), Schwaller meticulously examines many aspects of the temple at Luxor. Hidden in a strangely askew series of buildings or chambers at precisely the correct positions—as determined by overlays of the human skeleton—are brain and body outlines, the olfactory orifices, ear canals, eye openings, the twelve cranial nerves, brain structures, body organs and so forth. Yet this is only the beginning. What monumental intelligence it took to integrate everything incorporated in this monument to life!

West took seriously Schwaller's thought that the Sphinx was far older than the pyramid near which it is situated which has resulted in an Emmy-winning television show and considerable controversy (see the following article).

Both *Serpent...* and Lucie's *Egyptian Mysteries* (which is a fine introduction to West's work) contain over 100 photographs and drawings which illustrate how a symbol or a thought was represented in carvings or hieroglyphs.

Studying the photos is, in itself, interesting and enriching. Human-headed birds, jackal-headed humans, men with erect phalluses protruding from the navel area, humans with either two left or two right hands. In every case an important message is being conveyed. These strange-to-us means were utilized by the ancients to enable direct, immediate communication with the real consciousness of the intelligence-of-the-heart. Such intelligence, though common to us all, has been stunted by humanity's adherence to lesser and material values and by the unwholesome educational practices arising therefrom. It knows things directly, absolutely and without comparison. Hieroglyphs, allegory, symbol and myth (in the true sense of these terms) sidestep cerebral intelligence, which thinks by comparison. But the method of our higher intelligence is intuition and a higher teaching must appeal to and activate it. This is foreign to us, yet vital and alive in a way cerebral intelligence cannot appreciate.

The capacity to explore nature and oneself according to its subtle principles of action leads to super science and super people. These individuals can—and did—establish a social order that benefits all who function within it—from the point of view of each individual's psychological evolution. Clearly, the magnificent, enigmatic structures, the masterful sculptures, paintings, friezes, carvings—everything—could not have been accomplished with such elegance, grace, delicacy, intelligence and attention to detail if the artisans and laborers had not known and deeply felt that they themselves were individually benefited by their work in a way that exceeded mere care or satisfaction of the body. Here we may observe a true civilization, a real culture with an

actual understanding in which wisdom established a construc-
tive milieu for all citizens. Many may grimace at this, but, does
anyone seriously believe that societies such as those of today's
Western world could possibly last 5000 years on the good earth
we have poisoned?

Isha Schwaller de Lubicz gained extraordinary wisdom during her long life. An expert in hieroglyphics and Egyptian symbology, she wrote both non-fiction and novels about it. In *Her-
Bak: Egyptian Initiate*, she weaves an illuminating, exhilarating,
edifying story from the life of Her-Bak and the profound knowledge the masters of the temple of Karnak teach him. Even
though a novel, it's not "easy reading." Every day Her-Bak is challenged to learn something new that further breaks the bonds of
cerebral intelligence on his mentations and places him among
those who truly can understand. Understand what? Suffice it to
say, the subtle interaction of the forces of creation, the hierarchi-
cal organization of everything existing, the structure of our
psyche, the complete nature of our psychology and the essence
of the relationship between the natural realm and the organizing
principles according to which it continually comes into being.

We can learn with *Her-Bak*. At one point, we overhear a
master informing Her-Bak that: "The commonest error among
men is to think they are free..." As Her-Bak, we twinge, then dispute, rebut or reject. But with Her-Bak, wisdom prevails: in one
way he lived at a better time. We do appear to be slaves of our
cerebral intelligence with its remarkable capacity to form associ-
ations (habits) and to run our lives for us, we being typically unaware of all that's cooking. Indeed, in *Opening*...a goodly portion
of chapter three is devoted to a consideration of the "automa-
ton" and the existence of two independent wills in humans. Of
course, the brain, having gained ascendance through no fault of
its own, does not happily yield to the higher will. In those who
sustain the higher will, a duel results. This is inevitable and as it
must be. But why? R. A. explains in *The Egyptian Miracle*, the
Pharaonic mentality understood, "...that every phenomenon is a
reactive effect." Further, "A cause never produces a direct effect..." i.e., resistance is required for a force to have an effect, he
says. "Incomprehension of this idea is the basis of error in Western mentality." "Reaction," he says "is life." Absorption or non-

reaction annul a force, as can be seen clearly in martial arts.

All of these works concern humanity, our position in the universe and the fulfillment of our promise, our actual potential, through psychological evolution. Perhaps for many people today these topics do not command attention. Even so, many of the books can be read simply for intellectual enrichment. This is particularly true for *Serpent...* wherein West considers a broad array of subjects, quite often as their treatment today compares with their treatment by the Pharaonic sages. The process is intrinsically educational, interesting, and often inspiring. If one has any humility at all (it's not a value these days, is it?) one finds oneself in awe of what the sages did and conjecturing on the understanding they must have attained. Science, then, integrated everything—art, literature, philosophy, theology—into a unified, mutually related, internally consistent whole. This was not, as some think, because the Pharaonic sages knew less; it was because they knew and understood far more than we.

The truth of this ancient science can be verified and already some has. In a remarkable little book, *Esotericism and Symbol*, R. A. states, "Pictorial writing is the only means of conveying a thought directly to intelligence-of-the-heart." Hieroglyphs depend upon visual *gnosis*, they *evoke* innate consciousness and can "be translated thereafter by the cerebral intelligence." Is it not apparent here that hieroglyphs are "received" and understood by the right hemisphere which is known to be visually adept, synthetic in its operation and translated by the left hemisphere which is linguistic and analytic, working in its service? And did brain researchers not discover those different functions of the two hemispheres in the early '70s, which conform admirably to the requirements demanded by the language of the Pharaonic sages? (This book was actually written in 1947, but not published in French until 1960.)

By the way, R. A. tells us that our understanding of many key terms (such as symbol, esoteric) is now incomplete or worse. In turn, this increases the difficulty we have in coming simply to experience their form of thought: it is synthetic, not analytic; holistic, not fragmentary. It appears to be but is not authoritarian and absolutist. It is simply beyond rational thinking, sequential logic and the dualization essential to cerebrally based thought.

5

Getting Answers from the Sphinx

by J. Douglas Kenyon

First, they'll ignore you," observed John Anthony West, paraphrasing one of his favorite 19th century scholars, "then they'll laugh at you, then they'll say that everyone has known it all along. We're past the 'ignoring' stage. The NBC special saw to that."

West, an old-fashioned scholar/explorer in the tradition of Champollian or Heinrich Schliemann, is also a notorious thorn-in-the-side of what he calls the "church of progress—the essential dogma of which is that, via a sort of inexorable Darwinian process, we're the most advanced beings to have ever existed on the face of this planet..." He was reflecting on the progress of his own revolutionary theory on the origins of the great and mysterious Sphinx (at least 3,000 years older, and probably much more, than the 'experts' have claimed) and the uproar which his views have generated within the hallowed halls of academe.

When NBC aired "The Mystery of the Sphinx"—an hour-long documentary, narrated by Charleton Heston, which favorably reviewed the research and theories of West and Boston University geologist Dr. Robert Schoch—millions of viewers learned for the first time the details of what is developing into the hottest archeological controversy since Schliemann confounded the 'experts' by discovering Troy over a century ago. The show earned an

Reprinted from Atlantis Rising Magazine, issue #1.

Photo by Caroline Davies

Emmy for West for research, and a nomination for best documentary. Not surprisingly, the Egyptological establishment has
been at considerable pains to dispose of this very annoying matter. A lengthy cover article by West's chief antagonist, Dr. Zahi
Hawass, in *Archeology* struggles vainly to 'debunk' the West/
Schoch arguments. At stake is the carefully woven fabric of theories and assumptions upon which rests the academic authority of
today's reigning school of thought. Establishment scholars assert
that there was NO ancient civilization before dynastic Egypt, certainly not one capable of the kind of construction apparent in
the Sphinx and its associated temples. If West is right—that there
WAS a high but forgotten civilization which came long before
what we now call ancient Egypt—then a very great deal that we
have been taught is wrong and the implications may eventually
be felt in every corner of civilized life, in much the same way
that thought in Galileo's time was revolutionized by his notion of
a sun-centered planetary system—an idea which helped usher in
the Renaissance.

A writer and independent Egyptologist, John Anthony West,
has been studying and writing about ancient Egypt for nearly
thirty years. His best-known book *Serpent in the Sky* (first published in 1978) studied the work of Alsation philosopher R. A.
Schwaller de Lubicz who in the 1930s and '40s made an exhaustive effort to retrieve the lost wisdom of ancient Egypt. West was
particularly struck by Schwaller's observation that the Sphinx
had been weathered by WATER, not wind and sand—a very important point, considering that there has been no significant
rainfall in the area for at least 10,000 years. Realizing that here
was something—unlike many, more subjective, propositions—
which could be tested with hard science, he set out to prove the
point. After recruiting Schoch and other experts, an expedition
was mounted in 1992 to carry out on the Great Sphinx the extensive scientific and geological studies which were called for.
After months of hot and dusty observation and study about the
ancient structures of the Giza plateau, the result was a very compelling, albeit shocking, case—subsequently presented in the
NBC documentary and later in a BBC production.

Recently, West, in an interlude between cable TV production discussions and another trip to Egypt, spent some time shar-

ing views on the 'church of progress', the media, various pyramid theories and assorted other subjects. Throughout, the sometimes razor-tongued West never hesitated to speak his mind. Drawing him out was not the problem. The real challenge was keeping up with a virtual flood of rapid-fire, far-ranging and often surprising observations. The point was illustrated when a listener wanted to know if the Sphinx was the last great artifact of Atlantis.

"*Archeology Review* says, 'West believes the Sphinx was built by Atlantians who came from Mars,'" he chuckled. "I believe no such thing. I am however more and more convinced by a growing body of evidence of a vanished high civilization. Some of the best evidence was gathered around the turn of the century, when scholarship was really scholarship and it wasn't a kind of mutual admiration society by a bunch of ignorant Ph.Ds. There's a tremendous amount of evidence—including the legends and mythologies of the world that talk about vanished civilizations. I use 'Atlantis' simply because it's the best known of those theories. I'm sort of sorry that I talked about Egypt as a legacy of Atlantis in *Serpent in the Sky*, because I've had this thrown back at me, even though I'm very careful to use 'Atlantis' in inverted quotes, as, let's say, a name applied to some lost civilization. Whether in the middle of the Atlantic Ocean or the north pole or the south pole or whatever is immaterial. In other words, while I'm not saying the Sphinx is a relic of Atlantis as such, I am saying that the Sphinx was built by a prior high civilization, and I would not say that it's the ONLY artifact. It's the only sort of OBVIOUS artifact."

West is not surprised when opponents misrepresent his views. "Very often in breakthrough ideas the opposition is busy concocting disinformation and misinformation—often deliberately misinterpreting data in order to rebut a theory and preserve the status quo. And very often that policy works, because if you can confuse the issue sufficiently, you've absolutely baffled the layman who just gives up in despair and says it's too complicated for me. And it throws off the academics who are not immediately directly involved in the argument."

The process by which old ideas are replaced with new ones West sees as essentially political. Drawing from Machiavelli's observation on why it is difficult to initiate reform, he points out, "the opposition is united against the new idea, while those who believe in it are, for the most part, lukewarm and not willing to stick their necks out for it. It's only if the reformers have power on their side that they can actually see their ideas brought to fruition. Our power actually stems from the media. Without that we would have been stonewalled into total oblivion for decades or generations. Or maybe forever."

The media, West feels, has been quite responsible in its presentation of his theories: "For the most part, they've printed what we've had to say and they printed what the opposition had to say and left the matter for the readers to judge." Yet while recognizing the value of making an end run around the establishment through the press, West sees the course as not without risks: "courting the media is a bit like trying to satisfy a tiger by hand-feeding it steaks. You never know if you're going to get your arm chewed off...it's fortunate for us that we had the geologists behind us."

Though West is far from happy over the current state of civilization, he does discern a hopeful paradox. "We're in a peculiar position today," he muses. "Quite frankly, I think what I call the 'church of progress'—the reigning materialistic so-called rationalistic philosophy that rules the Western world and now, by extension, the rest of the world—is probably the biggest catastrophe to hit the human race since monogamy. Absolute disaster. However, within that disaster there is—for want of a better word—the miracle of mass communication and a tremendous amount of both scientific and scholarly inquiry that now makes it possible for the first time to actually retrieve the lost knowledge of the ancients."

The desirability of such a recovery, says West, was an article of faith for centuries, and even though pooh-poohed by modern academia, the idea has had great appeal to many of the most scientific minds of the last four or five hundred years. Kepler and Newton were among those who believed there was such an ancient knowledge, though they had no idea how to recover it. West believes that now, thanks to the work of Schwaller de Lubicz and others in modern scholarship and science, "it now becomes possible to understand what those ancient civilizations were all about."

And not a moment too soon. "I'm personally convinced," he says, "that for human beings to survive on this earth we need both individually and collectively a spiritual philosophy that allows us to do what Schwaller de Lubicz called "return to the source." We're born carnal and we have the possibility of becoming spiritual. And this is what all the religions—I don't care how horrific they now appear in their institutionalized form—have buried within their doctrines and their rules telling you what to eat and what to do with your body and who to marry and all the rest of the horrible stuff that they perpetrate. Within their doctrines there's always an esoteric core which is a return to the source." After a pause, he continues, "The religions we have today are in fact quite decadent and simple-minded versions of a much higher doctrine that existed not only in deep antiquity in terms of Egypt, India and China but that preexisted in still earlier civilizations. If we can look and see that we didn't go from dumb old cavemen to smart old us with our hydrogen bombs and our striped toothpaste and our traffic jams, but that we learned from civilizations already in place who knew, even from a technological standpoint, more than we knew, then that knowledge could be crucial in paving the way to something that resembles a real civilization. But if you asked me to delineate the practical step-by-step process by which this might manifest, I couldn't do it."

Though he says the idea of reincarnation "is not part of his personal experience," West is willing to consider that the past is accessible from within us individually. "There's too much evidence out there, as far as I'm concerned—and good concrete evidence—that says there's something to it. I tend to have a kind of rule of thumb, that if an idea is sufficiently old—which is to say pre-Aristotle—there's probably something to it. Reincarnation has a long history—but it's a little bit dangerous to use it for an explanation for anything that you don't understand. Like if you start saying that all of the Jews that were killed in the holocaust are reincarnated souls who used to be anti-semites, you can pretty much excuse any horrific acts that human beings commit upon each other. However, that we contain the past within us, yeah, I think so." West sees further indications of the proposition in his own position vis a vis the academic establishment. "We seem to be dealing with reincarnations of the astronomers who refused to look through Galileo's telescope."

West certainly respects the view that the planet's history is replete with catastrophic episodes. "There's a lot of physical evidence for this sort of stuff. Whatever caused the mammoth mammal extinction toward the poles in Siberia and equivalently in the southern hemisphere had to have been something of earth-shattering consequence. Just now we've seen that comet explode and blow into Jupiter, and any one of those pieces would have completely destroyed the earth. Catastrophism is a perfectly respectable scientific theory among the scientific elite, except when it is applied to relatively recent pre-history. I think catastrophism is a commanding idea and the scenario is simply that following such an event there weren't many people around to be the storytellers and the bards."

West believes the Great Pyramid itself was probably built by the pharaoh Cheops as most establishment Egyptologists claim, but he believes it may have been built over a preexisting structure of undetermined scale and antiquity. A Belgian engineer named Robert Bauval has impressed West with astronomical evidence indicating that while passages in the pyramid are apparently aligned with the constellation Orion in around 2450 B.C.— when the structure is purported to have been built—the arrangement of the three pyramids and the Sphinx on the Giza plateau appears to represent a configuration of stars that would have been present around 10,500 B.C. or even much earlier. West, however, does not believe the great pyramid was built as a tomb, and he cites a complete lack of evidence that they were ever used as such. "They're a total departure from the way Egyptian tombs were built both before and after. I think they may have had many purposes—among them that they served an initiatic (or ceremonial) purpose. They were placed where specific ceremonies were conducted for good reasons—very deep shamanic reasons—which correspond to the Egyptian metaphysical and spiritual philosophy. And they also may well have had specific astronomical purposes. And there was no such thing as astronomy in the ancient world without astrology." West hopes to have more to say on various mysteries associated with the pyramids on future television documentaries.

Most who saw the NBC documentary on the Sphinx project will remember intriguing questions raised by some of the research, most notably the seismic evidence of a possible chamber beneath the paws of the Sphinx. Would excavating such a chamber fulfill a prophecy by the famous clairvoyant Edgar Cayce? The answers to that and other questions such as: "What will a complete isotopic analysis reveal about the true age of the Sphinx?" await a future expedition. At the moment, plans for any such expedition are on hold. The authorities, say West, vehemently oppose any return by him and Schoch. One of the bitterest opponents, Zahi Hawass, holds a deciding vote on any proposals regarding the Sphinx and the Giza plateau. "If he were in a position of political power," says West, "I would never go near Egypt. He'd see to it that I was in a jail and never got out." Nevertheless, both West and Schoch believe that ultimately a way will be found to return. With pressure from the media building, especially after the BBC show, it is becoming increasingly difficult, they believe, to put the matter to rest, without a definitive and impartial analysis.

For the moment, West is content that he has launched a process which promises to fulfill a lifelong ambition. "Nowadays it's common for teenagers and just about everyone else to recognize that we live in a lunatic society," he says. "I take considerable credit for having recognized it at about the age of 11 or 12. By the time I was 19, I had set my goal. I thought I was going to devote my life to writing, but my real aim was to upset, in one way or another, the lunatic asylum. I never dreamed that it was going to take me into scholarship or Egypt—it wasn't even a particular subject of mine. But my aim always was to undermine the 'church of progress'. And funnily enough it looks as though, though it looked wildly ambitious when I was 19, we are sure producing some cracks in the facade. All of which pleases me enormously."

6

Fingerprinting the Gods
by J. Douglas Kenyon

Although few would question the popularity of *Raiders of the Lost Ark*, no academic worth his salt ever dared to say the movie was more than a Hollywood fantasy either. So when respected British author Graham Hancock announced to the world in 1992 that he had actually tracked the legendary Ark of the Covenant of Old Testament fame to a modern-day resting place in Ethiopia, serious eyebrows everywhere twitched upward. Nevertheless, objective readers of his monumental volume *The Sign and the Seal*, on both sides of the Atlantic, soon realized that Hancock's case, incredible though it seemed, was not to be easily dismissed. The exhaustively researched work went on to enjoy widespread critical acclaim, to become a best-seller in both America and the U.K. as well as to become the subject of several television specials.

Hancock's writing and journalistic skills had been honed during stints as a war correspondent in Africa for *The Economist* and *The London Sunday Times*. Winner of an honorable mention for the H. L. Mencken Award (*The Lords of Poverty*, 1990), he also authored *African Ark: Peoples of the Horn*, and *Ethiopia: The Challenge of Hunger*. In *The Sign And The Seal*, Hancock was credited by *The Guardian* with having "invented a new genre—an intellectual whodunit by a do-it-yourself sleuth...."

Reprinted from Atlantis Rising Magazine, issue #4.

Apparently, though, the success of *The Sign and the Seal* has only whetted the writer's appetite for establishment chagrin. In his latest book Hancock is out for even bigger game. In fact, *Fingerprints of the Gods* seeks nothing less than to overthrow the cherished doctrine taught in classrooms worldwide, that civilization was born roughly 5,000 years ago. Anything earlier, we are told, was strictly primitive. In one of the most comprehensive efforts on the subject ever—over 600 pages of meticulous research—Hancock presents breakthrough evidence of a forgotten epoch in human history which preceded by thousands of years the presently acknowledged cradles of civilization in Egypt, Mesopotamia and the Far East. Moreover, he argues, this same lost culture was not only highly advanced but technologically proficient and was destroyed more than 12,000 years ago by the global cataclysm which brought the ice age to its sudden and dramatic conclusion.

Just released in the U.S., *Fingerprints of the Gods* (Crown, 608 pp.), seeks to duplicate early successes in Great Britain where by mid-June it had already enjoyed considerable critical praise and six straight weeks as the number-one bestseller. *Kirkus Reviews* called it "a fancy piece of historical sleuthing—breathless, but intriguing and entertaining and sturdy enough to give a long pause for thought."

In America to promote *Fingerprints*, Hancock was at his hotel room in Washington, D.C. when *Atlantis Rising* caught up with him. With just two days of the tour behind him, it was still too early to estimate how the book would do here, but already he was enjoying the kind of favorable media attention which helped to make *The Sign and the Seal* an American hit. Interviewers, he felt, were generally positive and open to his ideas. While the reception among academics has been something less than cordial, that was to be expected. "One of the reasons the book is so long," he explained, "is because I've really tried to document everything very thoroughly, so that the academics have to deal with the evidence, rather than me as an individual, or with what they like to think are rather vague wishy-washy ideas. I've tried to nail it all down to hard fact as far as possible."

Nailing down the facts took Hancock on a worldwide odyssey which included stops in Peru, Mexico, and Egypt. Among the many intriguing mysteries which the author was determined fully to investigate were:

- Ancient maps showing precise knowledge of the actual coastline of Antarctica, notwithstanding the fact that the location has been buried under thousands of feet of ice for many millennia.

- Stone building technology—beyond our present capacity to duplicate—in Central and South America, as well as Egypt.

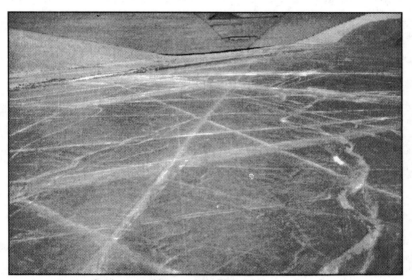

Ancient markings on the Plain of Nazca, Peru

- Sophisticated archeo-astronomical alignments at ancient sites all over the world.

- Evidence of comprehensive ancient knowledge of the 25,776-year precession of the equinoxes (unmistakably encoded into ancient mythology and building sites, even though the phenomenon would have taken, at a minimum, many generations of systematic observation to detect, and which conventional scholarship tells us was not discovered until the Greek philosopher Hipparchus in about 150 B.C.).

- Water erosion of the Great Sphinx dating it to before the coming of desert conditions to the Giza plateau (as researched by American scholar John Anthony West and geologist Robert Schoch).

Evidence that the monuments of the Giza plateau were built in alignment with the belt of Orion at circa 10,500 B.C. (as demonstrated by Belgian engineer Robert Bauval).

Unfettered as he is by the constraints under which many so-called specialists operate, Hancock sees himself uniquely qualified to undertake such a far-reaching study. "One of the problems with academics, and particularly academic historians," he insists, "is they have a very narrow focus. And as a result they are very myopic."

Hancock is downright contemptuous of organized Egyptology, which he places in the particularly short-sighted category. "There's a rigid paradigm of Egyptian history," he complains, "which seems to function as a kind of filter on knowledge and which stops Egyptologists, as a profession, from being even the remotest bit open to any other possibilities at all." In Hancock's view Egyptologists tend to behave like priests in a very narrow religion, dogmatically and irrationally, if not superstitiously. "A few hundred years ago they would have burned people like me and John West at the stake," he laughs.

Such illogical zealotry Hancock fears stands in the way of the public's right to know about what could be one of the most significant discoveries ever made in the Great Pyramid. In 1993, the German inventor Rudolph Gantenbrink sent a robot with a television camera up a narrow shaft from the Queen's chamber and discovered what appears to be a door with iron handles. That door, Hancock suspects, might lead to the legendary 'hall of records' of the ancient Egyptians. But whatever is behind it, he feels it must be properly investigated. So far, though, there has been no official action, at least not a public one. Citing episodes personally witnessed, he protests "you have Egyptologists saying 'there is no point in looking to see if there's anything behind that slab'—they call it a 'slab', they won't call it a door—'because we know there's not another chamber inside the great pyramid.' "The attitude infuriates Hancock, "I wonder how they know that, in this 6-million-ton monument which has got room for 3,000 chambers the same size as the king's chamber. How do they háve the temerity and the nerve to suggest that there's no point in looking?"

The tantalizing promise of that door has led Hancock to speculate that the builders may have purposely arranged things to require technology of ultimate explorers. "Nobody could get in there unless they had a certain level of technology." And he points out that even a hundred years ago we didn't have the means to do it. In the last 20 years the technology has been developed and now the shaft has been explored, "and lo and behold, at the end is a door with handles. It's like an invitation—an invitation to come on in, look inside, when you're ready."

Hancock is far from sanguine about official intentions. "If that door ever does get open, probably there will be no public access at all to what happens." He would like to see an international team present, but suspects that, instead, "what we're going to get is a narrow elite group of Egyptologists who will strictly control information about what happens." In fact, he thinks it's possible that they've even been in there already. The Queen's chamber was suspiciously closed for more than nine months after Gantenbrink made his discovery. "The story was given out that they were cleaning the graffiti off the walls but the graffiti was never cleaned off. I wonder what they were doing in there those nine months. There's what really makes me angry, that this narrow group of scholars control knowledge of what is at the end of the day the legacy of the whole of mankind."

Gantenbrink's door is not the only beckoning portal on the Giza plateau. Hancock is equally interested in the chamber which John Anthony West and Robert Schoch, in the course of investigating the weathering of the Sphinx, detected, by seismic methods, beneath the paws. Either location might prove to be the site of the "hall of records." In both cases, the authorities have resisted all efforts at further investigation.

Hancock believes the entire Giza site was constructed after the crust of the earth had stabilized following a 30-degree crustal displacement which destroyed most of the high civilization then standing. According to Rand and Rose Flem-Ath's *When the Sky Fell*, upon which Hancock relies, that displacement had moved an entire continent from temperate zones to the south pole where it was soon buried under mountains of ice. This, he believes, is the real story of the end of Plato's 'Atlantis,' but the 'A' word is not mentioned until very late. "I see no point in giving a hostile establishment a stick to beat me with," he offers. "It's purely a matter of tactics."

The Giza complex was built, Hancock speculates, as part of an effort to remap and reorient civilization. For that reason he believes the 10,500 B.C. date (demonstrated by Bauval) to be especially important. "The pyramids are a part of saying this is where it stopped. That's why the perfect alignment, for example, to due north, of the Great Pyramid is extremely interesting, because they obviously would have had a new north at that time."

Despite a determination to stick with the hard evidence, Hancock is not uncomfortable with the knowledge that his work is serving to corroborate the claims of many intuitives and mystics. On the contrary, he believes "that the (clairvoyant ability) of human beings is another one of those latent faculties which modern rational science simply refuses to recognize. I think we're a much more mysterious species than we give ourselves credit for. Our whole cultural conditioning is to deny those elements of intuition and mystery in ourselves. But all the indications are that these are, in fact, vital faculties in human beings, and I suspect that the civilization that was destroyed, although technologically advanced, was much more spiritually advanced than we are today."

Such knowledge, he believes, is part of the legacy of the ancients which we must strive to recover. "What comes across again and again, particularly from documents like the ancient Egyptian Pyramid texts, which I see as containing the legacy of knowledge and ideas from this lost civilization, is a kind of science of immortality—a quest for the immortality of the soul, a feeling that immortality may not be guaranteed to all and everybody simply by being born. It may be something that has to be worked for. Something that results from the focused power of the mind." The real purpose of the pyramids, he suggests, may be to teach us how to achieve immortality. But before we can understand, we must recover from the ancient amnesia.

Hancock believes we are a species with amnesia. "I think we

show all the signs that there's a traumatic episode in our past, which is so horrible that we cannot somehow bring ourselves to recognize it. Just as the victim suffering from amnesia as a result of some terrible episode fears awakening memory of that trauma and tries to avoid it, so we have done collectively." The amnesia victim is, of course, forced to return to the source of his pain and "if you wish to move forward and continue to develop as an individual you have to overcome it. You have to confront it, deal with it, see it face to face, realize what it means, get over it, and get on with your life. That is what society needs to be doing."

In the institutional resistance to considering ancient achievement, Hancock sees a subconscious pattern based on fear. "There's a huge impulse to deny all of this, because suddenly all the foundations get knocked out from under you and you find yourself swimming loosely in space without any points of reference anymore." The process needn't be so threatening though. "If we can go through that difficult experience and come out on the other side, I think we'll all emerge better from it. I'm more and more convinced that the reason we are so messed up and confused and totally disturbed as a species at the end of the 20th century is because of this—because we've forgotten our past."

If it is true that those who cannot learn from history are doomed to repeat it, then there are lessons in our past which can be ignored only at our peril. Clearly written into the mythology of many societies are stories of cataclysmic destruction. Hancock cites the work of Giorgio de Santillana, an authority on the history of science at M.I.T. In his book *Hamlet's Mill*, Santillana hypothesized that an advanced scientific knowledge was encoded into ancient myth. Hancock points out, "Once you accept that mythology may have originated with highly advanced people, then you have to start listening to what the myths are saying." What the myths are saying, he believes, is that a great cataclysm struck the world and destroyed an advanced civilization and a golden age of mankind. And the bad cataclysm is a recurrent feature in the life of the earth and will return. The messages from many ancient sources, including the Bible, point to a recurrence of such a cataclysm in our lifetime. Notwithstanding such views, Hancock insists he is not a prophet of doom. His point is, "We've received a legacy of extraordinary knowledge from the past, and the time has come for us to stop dismissing it. Rather, we must recapture that heritage, learn what we can from it, because there is vitally important information in it."

The stakes couldn't be higher. "I'm convinced that we're locked today in a battle of ideas," he says. "I think it's desperately important that the ideas that will lead to a recovery of our memory as a species triumph. And therefore we have to be strong, we have to be eloquent, and argue clearly and coherently. We have to see what our opponents are going to do, how they are going to try to get at us. And the dirty tricks that they are going to try and play. We have to fight them on their own ground."

Hancock's next book will be a collaboration with Robert Bauval in which he plans not only to complete the decoding of the archeo-astronomy of the Giza plateau, but also to protest the way official Egyptology has behaved. In the process, Hancock promises to air some of the establishment's dirty linen, "to look behind the scenes at what they've been doing—how research has been hindered, misled and misguided by a narrow group of scholars protecting their own interests at the cost of the rest of humanity. We have uncovered a really serious scandal in Egyptology which, once it's brought out into public view, will make it impossible for this group of scholars who have controlled Giza for the last 20 years to have any credibility at all."

In the meantime *Fingerprints of the Gods* promises to expose the academic authorities to a new level of enlightened public scrutiny.

7
Originators from Orion?
by Len Kasten

A ccording To Author-Astronomer Robert Bauval, the answer to the ancient secret of Giza is in the stars.

When Robert Bauval came to the realization, one starry night in the Arabian desert, that the three pyramids of Giza were arranged on the ground to replicate the arrangement of the three stars in Orion's belt, ancient astronaut theorization was the farthest thing from his mind. "Je tiens l'affaire," he shouted excitedly when he understood the connection, deliberately mimicking Champollion's exclamation when he had deciphered the Rosetta Stone. At the time of his discovery, Bauval was a construction engineer working in the Middle East. In his subsequent book, *The Orion Mystery*, co-authored with Adrian Gilbert, Bauval demonstrated convincingly that the ancient Egyptians were sophisticated astronomers, and that their religious beliefs and practices were far more profound and esoteric than previously believed. His thesis that the entire area of lower Egypt was laid out in emulation of the heavens is revolutionary, giving new meaning to the famous dictum of Hermes/Thoth, "As above, so below." Furthermore he, too, as had John Anthony West, Graham Hancock, and Edgar Cayce, pushed the frontiers of high Egyptian civilization way back to 10,500 B.C.

Bauval was born in Alexandria, Egypt to European parents,

Reprinted from Atlantis Rising Magazine, issue #5.

and has retained a fascination with his native country which eventually nagged him to find the real truth about ancient Egypt. Dissatisfaction with conventional Egyptology was evidently lurking in the back of his mind when, one day in 1979, at Heathrow Airport in London, he picked up a copy of Robert Temple's *The Sirius Mystery*. Temple showed that the African Dogon tribe had extremely ancient religious traditions centering around the Sirius star system. To Bauval, this suggested a connection with the ancient Egyptian traditions concerning Sirius, as well as the Orion star system. Thus began an investigative odyssey that culminated in one of the most important archeological discoveries of the 20th century. Many believe that before all of the ramifications of his breakthrough have played out, the stage will be set for a totally new understanding of our origins.

The Sphinx in the Sky
We met Bauval in July, 1995, at an A.R.E. conference in Virginia Beach subtitled "Atlantis Rising," (purely coincidental). He was the featured speaker. We asked about the debate over 2,500 B.C. vs. 10,500 B.C. "There is no doubt in my mind whatsoever that the pyramids of Giza were built, physically built, in 2,500 B.C. We can't escape that. The area is carbon-dated. But the knowledge of building it was known long, long before. I think that what you're looking at is a blueprint that finally took shape. And the blueprint originated in the period of 10,500 B.C." But consonant with the evidence cited by John Anthony West, Bauval believes that the Sphinx was indeed carved out in 10,500 B.C. However, while West arrived at this date geologically, Bauval used astronomy.

Astronomical correlations are at the very heart of Bauval's discoveries and theories. As an amateur astronomer, he has delved deeply into the connections, but many of them are obvious. In fact, it is nothing short of astounding that for over two hundred years now, Egyptologists have avoided the stellar implications. of ancient Egyptian beliefs and architecture, when it appears that their entire religious apparatus was based on the constellations. In his book, Bauval blames this on the longtime domination of Egyptology by one man, American James Henry Breasted, who adopted a monotheistic solar explanation which threw the star theory into disrepute.

Astrologers have long known about the 25,600-year cycle commonly referred to as the "Precession of the Equinoxes." Every 2160 years, the vernal point, moving along the ecliptic, enters a new sign of the zodiac, going backwards, due to the wobble of the earth. According to Manly Hall and others, each change of sign ushers in a new religio-philosophical dispensation. In *The Orion Mystery*, Bauval makes the bold claim that the ancient Egyptian astronomer-priests knew about precession as early as 10,500 B.C., which was the time that the constellation of Orion was at its lowest point on the meridian, and therefore started its upward cycle. This would be incredible, if true, because it means they would have had to carefully observe star movements, without telescopes, for thousands of years. The importance of Orion to the ancient Egyptians is, of course, well known from the Pyramid Texts, as the home of Sahu, or "Osiris in the sky." In our conversation, Bauval elaborated on this, pointing out how precession was used. "At 10,500 B.C. when the constellation of Orion is at the low point, it also happens to be crossing the meridian at the time of the vernal equinox. On that day, the vernal point would be due East. That immediately draws your attention to the Sphinx, because the Sphinx looks due East. And when you investigate the position of that vernal point at 10,500 B.C. you'll find that it is exactly between Virgo and Leo. The constellation was performing its first heliacal rising. This means that the Age of Leo was just beginning. Now, this coincidence is a million to one. It's luring us to consider that the image of the Sphinx is a symbol of the lion in the sky—Leo. The message is...'look at the Age of Leo.'"

So, according to Bauval, the Sphinx was built to establish the advent of the Age of Leo as a marker in precessional time, and to identify it for future ages as what the Pyramid Texts call the "first time." Then, says Bauval, 8000 years later, the pyramid builders gave us further evidence that the plan was first hatched at 10,500 B.C. The arrangement of the Giza pyramids with respect to the Nile doesn't quite match the pattern in the stars and milky way at 2,500 B.C. But if the star map is rotated about 30 degrees to conform to the stellar pattern at 10,500 B.C., it matches perfectly. Bauval says, "My conclusion about Giza is that we're certain that it is a collective marker of Leo. They're both linked, but if you look at it in 2,500 B.C. it doesn't match. You're looking at the wrong time. The time that it's telling you to look at is 10,500 B.C. Now, how you explain that it took shape at 2,500 B.C. is another matter. But, it did."

Roadmap for a Time Journey

In his book Bauval points out that the importance of the Pyramid Texts, the oldest extant religious writings on the planet, has been trivialized by Breasted and the Egyptology "establishment." But, properly understood, he says, they provide the key to the symbology and purpose of Giza. He says, "There is a link between the pyramid texts and the pyramids, i.e., what one is saying textually, the other is saying architecturally, and we've proved this beyond any doubt. We begin to understand that the Pyramid Texts are not mumbo-jumbo at all. The message tells us that we are dealing with a dual landscape, two horizons. That is why the Egyptologists have missed out in finding the Sphinx in the Pyramid Texts—because the Texts speak of the Sphinx and the pyramids in cosmic terms. When they mention Orion, they mean the pyramids. When they mention 'horacty,' they mean the Sphinx. Once you understand this trick you can make the correlations from the cosmic to the terrestrial."

Once these masked references in the Pyramid Texts are deciphered, they can be seen as a sort of travel guide, or triptik, for Horus, the dead king, as he makes his way back to rejoin his father Osiris, in the stars. But his journey is not only through space. According to Bauval, it is also a time journey. "What we've recently discovered is that in Egypt in 10,500 B.C. there was a group of people called 'The Followers of Horus,' who were supposed to be ancestors of the kings, and their job was literally to follow Horus as he changed position, in order to know exactly where they were in time—in order to be able to return. The Pyramid Texts speak of the time of the original Osiris, and of the original Horus. They believed that there is a lineage of kings that emerges from this "first time," and that the king is supposed to return back to his origins in time. So basically the king uses the Followers of Horus to travel back. And the flux that he travels on is precession. That's why precession is built into this ancient architecture. They give us the date 2,500 B.C. with the Great Pyramid shaft pointing to Orion's belt, and then they tell us 'travel back in time.'"

A Science of Immortality

So far, Bauval had given us some fascinating new insights into the ancient Egyptian star religion, but had drawn no inferences. But at this point, the interview took an unexpected turn, as Bauval entered some new and daring territory. We asked him what sort of people could have designed such an elaborate and complex plan stretching out over 8,000 years with the confidence that it would come to fruition. "We're looking at a scientific way of thinking that is totally alien to us. It seems that we have a device that was built to work with time. It's a sort of calendar that these people, the Followers of Horus, built in order to be able to trigger certain events in the future. One of the things that they knew would happen, and they timed it, was the Pyramid Age.

"The Egyptians believed that certain individuals came from a divine origin, and these individuals had the ability to return to where they came from. There is something that we haven't yet quite understood about our capabilities. Because we feel uncomfortable with it, we use words like 'spirit,' 'soul,' 'intellect,' whatever. But there is something about us that may possibly be able to travel in time or in space. Now these people seemed to know about it, and they went to a lot of trouble to create a condition that somehow allowed this to happen. We call it ritual, we call it initiation. You can call it what you like. But they seemed to think that it was only possible to achieve it through a certain condition when the harmonics were right—when everything was right. It has something to do with stone; it has something to do with scale; it has something to do with a mental state. You have to be able to take yourself to the threshold of a journey—and the journey seems to be returning to a time when immortality was known."

This explanation seemed to approach Edgar Cayce's claim that the Great Pyramid was a temple of initiation. We asked him to elaborate on this, and his reply was surprising. "We seem to be dealing with people who were convinced that they had a science of immortality, and they built something that they felt was a device to achieve it."

Bauval was obviously referring to the priests at Heliopolis. But his description of their activities and goals strayed far from conventional Egyptology. "What I think happened here is that we have a very powerful nucleus, a messiah-making academy, if you like, at Heliopolis, that maintained the origin of an idea, maintained something, whether it's in physical form, whether it's the Hall of Records, whatever. They were the keepers of it. And they maintained it to a point where they finally were able to physically create a place for it to rest forever. My impression, based on the evidence, is that we're dealing with people who seemed to know their origins—who knew where they came from, literally, and they wanted to maintain this knowledge of their origins forever, never to be lost. They seemed to have been able to keep it for a long period of time, and finally found, perhaps within their own academy, or outside, an individual who could wield the nation in order to build what they had in mind, to find a repository for this knowledge of origins. There were 2,000 - 3,000 years of preparation for something to happen. And then it does happen. They find the right guy—they find the right moment. And the point in time is 2,500 B.C. And then their mission was accomplished, and they left."

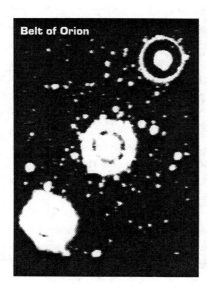

Belt of Orion

Giza pyramids from the air

The Gods of Orion

By this time, Bauval had used the "a" word (alien) twice, in other contexts, and he was now clearly advancing towards "Stargate" country. Although there are no ancient astronaut implications in his book, it was beginning to appear that he may have now begun to think about it, so we decided to turn the conversation in that direction. His response was startling, and placed his entire body of research and theory into a totally new domain. His answers put the capstone on his discovery, and suddenly it all made perfect sense. We could see that this was obviously not just an add-on idea, but was seamlessly integrated into his theoretical framework.

Bauval first argued that the Pyramid Texts were directing the dead king specifically to a place underneath the Sphinx. "We are led to conclude that by following the instructions, we reach a date of 10,500 B.C., and that somewhere underneath the Sphinx, somewhere between the Sphinx and the Great Pyramid, is something that has to do with 10,500 B.C. I'm translating the message as it is written in the Pyramid Texts, and on the monuments. And he's supposed to arrive at the region called "horacty" when he's finished his journey. And there he's arrived at the "time of the gods," and this is declared to be the place of the "first time." What he's told then is that when he reaches here, he's at the entrance of the necropolis. And now comes the terrestrial journey. It's said that now at this entrance he has to find the astral body of his father, of Osiris. So from here, he has to go to the pyramids, which are behind him, which we know represent the astral body of. Osiris. But he is actually told to go under the Sphinx. The message is to find the astral body which is behind you, you have to proceed to that point. And what we find there is a plaque in front of the Sphinx—a stele. And on it is written, 'This is the place of the first time.' Surprisingly, nobody has picked up its meaning."

The time had now come to ask the obvious question—the key question; what were the origins that the priests were so jealously guarding? Where did they come from? We pointed out to Bauval that the configuration of the three pyramids in replication of the Orion stars was only obvious from the sky. That observation elicited the following amazing reply. "What they are telling us, whether we like it or not, is that the gods came from the sky, and one of them, the major one, came from Orion. And they're telling us that in 10,500 B.C. they buried the body of Orion at Giza. And they're leading us on just enough, but making it hard to find. It isn't Robert Bauval that is saying this. The message is there."

When Bauval made that statement, the words of Von Daniken and Sitchin flashed through our mind. All of a sudden, it all made sense—the Nazca Plain, Machu Pichu, and Teotechaun. What makes Bauval's conclusion so convincing is the route by which he got there. He didn't start out with the extraterrestrial hypothesis, but arrived at it after a painstaking study of the Pyramid Texts, and a corresponding highly scientific astronomical study of the monuments. The body of evidence is there for anyone to see. 10,500 years before Christ, some super intelligent beings knew all about precession and galactic astronomy, and all the dimensions of the planet, and they laid out a construction plan on earth to duplicate the star patterns in order to leave behind an indestructible message telling us where they came from—and perhaps, where we came from!

The Galileo Syndrome

Having now revealed his entire message, Bauval felt free to comment on the extraordinary resistance to these ideas by the establishment, archeologists and Egyptologists, who refuse to even consider the star theory, and who have even been accused of suppressing some important new discoveries.

"There are a few of us who are trying to maintain the tempo, and what we're finding is the quintessential adversarial situation. There is enormous resistance.

"We're dealing with something that is giving us a cosmic address, a cosmic time, and it's screaming a message out loud. It's plain to read, but we won't accept it. And we feel uncomfortable with something that we shouldn't feel uncomfortable with. We live in a cosmic environment that cries out for us to consider an outer space explanation. This planet may very well have been visited. So, we may look like a bunch of fools now. But if we don't speak up, in two or three generations' time they'll say 'Well, the evidence was staring them in the face. They had these big things there. They were obviously astronomical. There was obviously something to investigate, and these idiots have concluded that they were tombs!'

"If there is any faint possibility that these people knew something that we don't know about our origins, let alone immortality, then we should pursue it, whatever the uncomfortable feeling we have. I can tell you that I am speaking far more openly now than I would have two years ago. But we're dealing with something of a scale and magnitude that has to be taken with the utmost seriousness."

Readers who found this article of interest should keep an eye open for Robert Bauval's next book, *Keepers of the Genesis*, currently being co-written with Graham Hancock, author of the very popular *Fingerprints of the Gods*. From the title, it is obvious that you have just read a preview of the book.

8

Hall of Records: Opening Soon?

by Dr. Joseph Jochmans, Litt.D.

Recently, archaeologists announced an important find has been brought to light—a major series of tombs found in the Valley of the Kings, the burial vaults of the sons of Ramses II. What is amazing is that previously, the Valley had been thoroughly searched for almost a century, and was thought to be completely exhausted for any further investigation. That a find of such major proportions could have eluded so many Egyptologists—including Howard Carter, the discoverer of the tomb of Tutankhamen in the same Valley, goes to show that the land of the Nile still has many secrets. What else, we may well ask, lurks below the sands?

For untold centuries both historical and esoteric sources have passed down stories of a forgotten time-capsule of Ancient Wisdom—far greater in importance than the golden treasures of Tutankhamen. The various accounts speak of chambers located beneath the Great Pyramid and the Sphinx at Giza, filled with a technological legacy left by lost advanced civilizations older than Egypt itself. Along with the stories are also preserved a number of prophecies foretelling who, when and how the vanished time-capsule will be opened.

The Messages in Stone

Our search begins with several stone stelae or tablets from

Reprinted from Atlantis Rising Magazine, issue #4.

the Middle and New Kingdom periods (between 4,000 and 3,000 years old), found in the vicinity of the Sphinx, which show the great animal reclining on top of a high pedestal surmounted by a cornice. One ancient artist, a Twelfth Dynasty scribe named Mentu-her, made sure his viewers knew his subject matter was the Great Sphinx and not other sphinxes found along the Nile, by drawing in the Pyramids in perspective in the background, a technique very rarely seen in Egyptian art.

Stele of Mentu-her

Seven other stelae go further, and show a door on the side of the pedestal. The famous Stele of Thutmose IV, located between the paws of the Sphinx, likewise depicts at its top the Sphinx lying upon an understructure, with a doorway clearly seen. Finally, on yet another stele, made by an official named Nezem, and now kept in the Louvre, there is clearly depicted a flight of six steps leading to the door.

Stele of Thutmose IV

Conservative scholars have attempted to explain the pedestal as simply a representation of the nearby Temple of the Sphinx, because from a front view perspective the Sphinx does look like it sits on its roof. But this illusion can only be seen from the front and on the surface. The ancient artists, on the other hand, depicted the pedestal from the side and from below.

In the 1930s, the sands around the Sphinx were finally completely cleared away, and we now know that the ancient monument rests firmly on bedrock. But the bedrock itself may have been the pedestal the Egyptian artists had in mind. And deep below somewhere along the southern side may yet be discovered the six steps and doorway, the entrance to secret hollowed-out chambers undisturbed.

An important early Egyptian source that tells us much about the Hall of Records is called the Building Texts, found among the hieroglyph inscriptions on the inner enclosure wall of the temple of Horus at Edfu, in the heart of southern Egypt. The Building Texts refer to a number of now lost documents, grouped together into what was called "The Sacred Book of Temples," which gave a history and description of the major shrines along the Nile from a very remote period. These were first established by a group of creator-entities called the Shebtiw, who were associated with the god "Divine Heart" or Thoth, the Egyptian deity of Wisdom.

According to the Building Texts, the sacred books and power objects were eventually placed back inside the bw-hmn or Hall, and the Shebtiw sealed the entrance, constructed a new "enclosure" about it, and erected power staffs and pillars outside to protect its secrets, hidden away again from all but its guardians. The site thereafter became known as bw-hmr, "the Place of the Throne of the Soul," regarded as the location where only the highest Initiations were performed.

In another Egyptian text, known today as the Westcar Papyrus, which bears evidence of dating to the Fourth Dynasty, is the story of an enigmatic sage named Djeda who could not only perform miraculous feats of magic, but who also possessed certain information concerning what he called "the secret chambers of the books of Thoth." In the narrative, Djeda told Pharaoh Khufu the location of specific keys that will one day open the hidden place, which he described as follows: In the city of Ani (Heliopolis) is a temple called the "House of Sapti," referring to Septi, the fifth Pharaoh of the First Dynasty, who reigned about 3000 B.C. Within the temple is a special library room where the scrolls of inventory are kept. The walls of this room are made of sandstone blocks, and either within or behind one of these blocks is a secret niche containing a small box made of flint or whetstone. It is within this box that the *ipwt*-seals or keys that will open the secret chambers of Thoth, the Hall of Records, may still be hidden.

When Khufu asked Djeda to bring these keys to him, the sage replied he did not have the power to do so, but prophesied that he who some day would find the keys would be one of *three* sons born to Rad-dedet, the wife of the chief priest of Ra in Heliopolis, Lord of Sakhbu (the second Lower Egyptian nome or district in the Nile Delta), and that the three would be born on the 15th day of the month of Tybi (our October-November).

Now it is generally interpreted that the three mentioned were the first three Pharaohs of the succeeding Fifth Dynasty. But because much of Egyptian literature is multi-leveled in its symbolism, there is reason to believe that a more hidden meaning may have been intended, that the three enigmatic "brothers" may also be those yet future individuals who will one day find and open the Hall of Records.

Today, many portions of the old city of Heliopolis are still

buried and unexcavated, silently resting underneath the expanding suburbs of Cairo. The secret of the House of Septi may yet
await discovery.

Ancient Tales

Interpreter of ancient languages Zecharia Sitchin cites a
hymn composed in the Eighteenth Dynasty which speaks of the
god Amun taking on the functions of the heavenly Harakhty (the
Sphinx) who attains "perception in his heart, command on his
lips" as he "enters the two caverns which are under his (the
Sphinx's) feet." The command of Amun is then placed into the
"writings of Thoth," the god of Hidden Knowledge and
Initiation.

The famed Greek historian Herodotus, in 443 B.C., recorded
after his visit to Egypt that extending beneath and in all directions far beyond the "pyramid whereon great figures are graven"
is a vast "labyrinth," and a "way into it underground."

In the Corpus Hermeticum—a body of treatises compiled
from older materials toward the beginning of the Christian era—
we find in one of these works, the "Virgin of the World," these
words:

"The sacred symbols of the cosmic elements, the secrets of
Osiris, were hidden carefully. Hermes (the Greek equivalent to
Thoth), before his return to Heaven, invoked a spell on them,
and said, "O holy books which have been made by my immortal
hands, by incorruption's magic spell remain free from decay
throughout eternity and incorrupt by time. Become unseeable,
unfindable, from everyone whose foot shall tread the plains of
this land, until old Heaven shall bring instruments for you,
whom the Creator shall call His souls. Thus spake he, and laying
the spells on them by means of his works, he shut them safe
away in their rooms. And long has been the time since they were
hid away."

The Roman Marcellinus, in the 4th century, stated: "There
are certain subterranean galleries and passages full of windings
beneath the pyramids which, it is said, the adepts in the ancient
rites (knowing that the flood was coming, and fearing that the
memory of the sacred ceremonies would be obliterated), constructed vaults in various places, mining them out of the ground

with great labor. And upon leveled walls they engraved the hieroglyphic characters."

Marcellinus' contemporary, Iamblichus, wrote a treatise on the Mysteries of the Egyptians, and described the Initiation associated with the Sphinx. In a secret location between the paws of the feline monument, he said, is a bronze door, its opening triggered by a hidden spring. Beyond it, the neophytes went into a circular room. From this point on, they were subject to a series of trials to become full members among the Initiates, eventually reaching Masterhood.

In similar fashion, the tenth century Coptic chronicler Al Masudi observed from earlier accounts that in the area of the Sphinx were subterranean doorways to the Giza monuments: "One entered the pyramid through a vaulted underground passage 100 cubits or more long; each pyramid had such a door and entry."

In later centuries, the medieval Arab chronicler Firouzabadi noted that the chambers of the Sphinx were constructed at the same time as the Great Pyramid: "The Pyramid was erected by Esdris (Hermes or Thoth), to preserve there the sciences, to prevent their destruction. And also, the first priests, by observations of the stars, preserved records of medicine, magic and talismans elsewhere." Likewise, Ibn Abd Alhokim, who told the story of the antediluvian king Salhouk's dream of the Flood and his building of the Pyramid to save wisdom, also recounted that Salhouk dug a vault nearby the Pyramid, filling it with all manners of works on mathematics, astronomy and physics: "And they built gates (entrances) of it forty cubits underground," with foundations "of massive stones from the Ethiopians, and fastened them together with lead and iron." When Salhouk was finished, "he covered it with colored marble from top to bottom and he appointed a solemn festival, at which were present all the inhabitants of the kingdom."

The Jewish historian Josephus recorded further that Enoch built an underground temple of nine vaults, one beneath the other, placing within tablets of gold. His son, Methuselah, also worked on the project, putting in the brick walls of the vaults according to his father's plan. As Manly P. Hall noted, the Freemasons predict that someday a man will locate this buried vault, and that he will be "an initiate after the order of Enoch."

Prophetic Code

Ever since two centuries ago when Sir Isaac Newton took a special interest in the sacred geometry of the Great Pyramid, and speculated that its inner labyrinth of tunnels and chambers was a "prophecy calendar in stone," a host of scholars have attempted to elaborate on this idea, and crack the Pyramid's prophetic code.

In correlation with the prophecy inside the Great Pyramid, the nearby Sphinx may hold its own symbology of past and future happenings. According to ancient Egyptian and Coptic traditions, one of the earlier forms of the Sphinx, before it was carved into its present configuration, is that it had the front paws of a lion, the back legs and tail of a bull, the face of a human, and along its sides where today one can see the remains of stone incendiary boxes, fires were lit at night to give the Sphinx the appearance of having the flaming wings of an eagle.

Lion. Bull. Human. Eagle. We have here not only the Four Beings before the throne of the Divine as described in the Books of Ezekiel and the Revelation, but we also have here the four Fixed signs of the Zodiac—Leo, Taurus, Aquarius and Scorpio.

Most significantly, in the Precession of the Equinoxes, the distant Age of Leo 12,000 years ago saw the burial of the Hall of Records beneath the Sphinx's front paws. Recent archaeological and geologic surveys conducted by John Anthony West and Robert Schoch have demonstrated that the Sphinx does indeed date to such a remote time period.

Today we have just entered the Age of Aquarius—and the face of the Sphinx symbolizes the face of global humanity joined in one mind and one heart, the goal of evolving Aquarian civilization.

Another 6,000 years into the future will complete the Sphinx's prophecy in the distant Age of Scorpio, when perhaps humanity's spiritual evolution will be complete. The flaming wings of the Sphinx may be more than just that of an eagle; they may signify the fire of the Phoenix, the higher form of Scorpio that epitomizes its central themes of death and transfiguration. It is striking to note that the Pyramid's time line ending in the 83rd century will also fall in the Age of Scorpio.

Another theory sees the Sphinx embodying not only the four Fixed signs, but more specific astrological locations which Philip Sedgwick in his book Astrology of Deep Space identifies as the Four Points of Avatar, found at 14 degrees of Leo, Taurus, Aquarius and Scorpio. There are those students of the Egyptian Mysteries who believe that when all Four Points of Avatar will be triggered by planetary configurations, this may be a cosmic key for opening the doorway into the Sphinx's forgotten secrets.

Significantly, the next occurrence will take place on August 6, 1999. Will this presage the opening of the hidden Hall of Records? After that, the only other Four Points of Avatar hits to take place in the foreseeable future will be from May 4-14, 2003; November 6-11, 2005; and January 2-10, 2006.

The Visionaries

America's most famous psychic, Edgar Cayce, who lived from 1877 to 1945, saw in vision that at the same time the Great Pyramid was being built over 12,000 years ago, other activities were underway to preserve books of knowledge. The hiding place for these books Cayce variously described as the hall of records yet to be uncovered, a storehouse of records, a time-capsule, a small tomb or pyramid, the pyramid of unknown origins as yet, the holy mount yet to be uncovered. As to which direction from the Sphinx the Hall lies, the seer specified in several trances that it is between that monument and the Nile river— toward the east—"as the sun rises from the waters, the line of the shadow (or light) falls between the paws of the Sphinx."

Renowned as France's most famous seer, Nostradamus in 1558 published the completed edition of his book of prophecies, *Les Vrayes Centuries*, The True Centuries. The book was composed of 969 prophetic quatrains or four-lined poetic verses, all purposely written cryptically as a defense against the Inquisition of his day, who took a dim view of all forms of forecasting.

Despite the obscuring of his words, many of Nostradamus' prophetic verses have seen their fulfillment to a remarkable degree of accuracy, describing such twentieth century events as the World Wars, the landing of a man on the Moon, and even such modern happenings of the 1990s as the fall of Communism

in Russia, the end of the Cold War, the Gulf War, the reunifica-
tion of Germany, plus the rise of global pollution and the AIDS
epidemic.

Nostradamus also left behind a significant group of verses
which—once we work out the seer's puzzling cryptics—offers us
invaluable information about the coming opening of the lost Hall
of Records in Egypt.

Here's one example:

*"They will come to discover the hidden topography of the
land (at Giza),*
*The urns holding wisdom within the monuments (the
Pyramids) opened up,*
*Their contents will cause the understanding of holy
philosophy to expand greatly,*
*White exchanged for black, falsehoods exposed, new
wisdom replacing the established tradition that no longer
work*

VII,14.

The Message from the Past to the Future

When we look at the sum total of information from both historical and psychic sources regarding the Hall of Records, we
find some remarkable correlations. These include: its location
(below and around the Sphinx), age (at least twelve millennia
old), identity of its builder (Thoth-Hermes), purposes (a storehouse and Initiation site), descriptions of its contents (advanced
wisdom and science), the number of its future openers (three),
the circumstances of its re-discovery (found by spiritual intuition), and the coming time-frame when it could possibly be
brought to light (between 1999 and 2012).

Most modern conservative Egyptologists believe that the Hall
of Records is nothing more than a mere myth or fable, because
its existence does not fit into currently "acceptable" views of ancient history. Yet the stubborn persistence of the story of the
lost Hall through the millennia, plus the consistency of its description and the integrity of the many sources testifying to its
reality, suggests there is something very substantial to the story,
that it may be based on fact. Perhaps very soon—within the next
fifteen years if the prophecies are right—we will be able to agree

with Egyptologist Gerald Massey, who wrote: "Someday what we thought was myth will be found to contain the true history of the past, while what we always regarded as history will be relegated to a myth of our own making."

Finding of the Hall of Records will no doubt catalyze the transformation of everything we know about the past—and in so doing, will also revolutionize how we will enter the future ahead. The lost time-capsule from the past may be destined to change the very nature of time itself, as we know it.

9

How Old Is the Great Pyramid, Really?
by Dr. Joseph Jochmans, Litt.D.

T he controversy raised by John Anthony West and Robert
Schoch concerning the true age of the Great Sphinx is now
beginning to overcast the other famous monuments which share
space on the Giza plateau—namely, the three pyramids that were
supposedly built by Pharaohs Khufu, Khafre and Menkhare in
the Fourth Dynasty. Were these Pyramids constructed only
4,300 years ago, or—like the Sphinx—is there evidence they
could be far older, dating instead to perhaps 12,000 years ago?

Let's begin first with looking at the age of the Great Pyramid.
The conservative historians' entire case for dating the Great Pyramid to the Fourth Dynasty rests upon two major pieces of evidence. The first is the story of Herodotus, who in 443 B.C. visited Egypt and recounted how Pharaoh Cheops (the Greek name
for Khufu) built the Great Pyramid during his reign with 100,000
men in 20 years. However, we now know this story is highly
questionable. Even his contemporaries called Herodotus the "Father of Lies." Not only do the construction estimates he gave not
work, but Herodotus, as an Initiate in the Egyptian Mystery
Schools, was sworn to secrecy regarding the true nature of the
Pyramid, and he more than likely copied a fictitious tale about
the monument that was then in circulation among the common
masses. The Greek historian's account stands in sharp contrast

Reprinted from Atlantis Rising Magazine, issue #8.

to most other Egyptian, Hebrew, Greek, Roman, Hermetic, Coptic and medieval Arabic scholarly sources which agree that the Great Pyramid was not constructed during the time frame of Pharaoh Khufu or Dynastic Egypt, but was the product of the "Age of the Gods" thousands of years earlier.

The second piece of evidence is the existence of painted hieroglyphic inscriptions found in the air space chambers above the King's Chamber, which include the name of Pharaoh Khufu. They were supposedly discovered by Col. Richard Howard-Vyse in 1837, when he forced his way up to these chambers using gunpowder. But there are certain facts showing these inscriptions were in actuality forgeries.

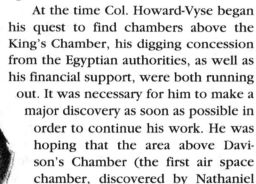

Col. Howard-Vyse

At the time Col. Howard-Vyse began his quest to find chambers above the King's Chamber, his digging concession from the Egyptian authorities, as well as his financial support, were both running out. It was necessary for him to make a major discovery as soon as possible in order to continue his work. He was hoping that the area above Davison's Chamber (the first air space chamber, discovered by Nathaniel Davison in 1765) would contain a large, hidden room or vault, and was severely disappointed when instead he brought to light only another air space chamber, which was far from the "dramatic discovery" he needed.

Only two months before, his rival, the Italian explorer Captain Caviglia, had stirred archaeological circles with his find of quarry inscriptions in some of the tombs around the Great Pyramid. These quarry inscriptions took the form of hieroglyphs daubed on the building blocks with a red paint, and had been used by the builders of the Old Kingdom as directions for where the blocks were to be placed. A number of modern researchers now suspect that, in the battle for archaeological oneupmanship, Col. Howard-Vyse sought to overshadow Caviglia, and gain renewed support for his own projects, with a similar but more spectacular "discovery," by imitating these quarry inscriptions inside the Great Pyramid itself. Forging such inscriptions would have been fairly easy, since the Arabs still use similar red ochre paint, called *moghrah*, that is indistinguishable from that of the ancients.

The question has never been answered, why do inscriptions appear only in the air space chambers that Col. Howard-Vyse opened, but none were found in Davison's Chamber, with which the Colonel had nothing to do, discovered earlier, in 1765?

Serious problems also arise when we examine the nature of the inscriptions themselves. Samuel Birch, a hieroglyph expert of the British Museum, was among the first to analyze the air chamber paintings, and noted a number of peculiarities among them which remain unresolved to this day. These "peculiarities" represent serious mistakes on the part of the forger. Birch noted, for example, that many of the daubings were not hieroglyphic but hieratic. Now hieratic was a form of written shorthand first developed during the Middle Kingdom, or at least a thousand years after the Fourth Dynasty. In one location, directly after a royal cartouche, the title is given, "Mighty in Upper and Lower Egypt," in a form that made its first appearance during the Saitic period of the 6th century B.C., a full 2,000 years after Khufu's reign.

"Khufu"
Cartouche

In another place, the hieroglyph symbol for "good, gracious" was used as the number "18," a usage found nowhere else in the entire body of Egyptian literature. In fact, Birch and later Egyptologists such as Carl Richard Lepsius and Sir Flinders Petrie were disturbed at the number of exceptions of usage in the air space chamber, inscriptions found by Col. Howard-Vyse that have absolutely no parallel throughout 4,000 years of hieroglyphic writing.

In perhaps the most blatant example of forgery, in Col. Howard-Vyse's chambers one finds great confusion concerning the appearance of the name Khufu. At the time these chambers were being opened, the Pharaoh's cartouche had not yet been fully revealed from other excavations, and there were several possibilities to choose from. As a result, a number of crude hybrid forms appear throughout the air chambers, such as "Khnem-Khuf," "Souphis," "Saufou," etc. The problem with the first example, "Khnem-Khuf," is that we know today that it signifies "brother of Khufu" and refers to Khafre, Khufu's eventual successor. For years, this appearance of a second king's name has not been explained, and as Gaston Maspero observed in *The Dawn of Civilization:* "The existence of the two cartouches of Khufu and Khnem-Khufu on the same monument has caused much embarrassment to Egyptologists."

Adding to this further is the fact that, where the right hieroglyph name for Khufu does appear, it is spelled wrong. The hieroglyph sources available to Col. Howard-Vyse in 1837, Sir John Gardner Wilkinson's *Material Hieroglyphia,* and Leon de Laborde's *Voyage de l'Arabee* Petree, incorrectly depicted the first symbol of Khufu's name as an open circle with a dot in the middle—the sign of Ra, the sun god—instead of a solid disk, which is the phonetic sound *kh.* Col. Howard-Vyse made the fatal error of copying this mistake in the uppermost of the air space chambers, so that, when strictly translated, the name given is Raufu, and not Khufu. Again, nowhere else in all of Egyptian literature, except in the air space chamber inscriptions, is this aberrant spelling for Khufu found.

This last mistake is the final blow showing that Col. Howard-Vyse and not the original builders of the Great Pyramid was the true source who caused the red-painted markings to be inscribed. And with that the proof that the Great Pyramid was built by Pharaoh Khufu in the Fourth Dynasty also vanishes.

Actually, we have the testament of Pharaoh Khufu himself that he only did repair work on the Great Pyramid. The Inventory Stele, found in 1857 by Auguste Mariette just to the east of the Pyramid, dates to about 1500 B.C., but according to Maspero and other experts, shows evidence of having been copied from a far older stele contemporaneous with the Fourth Dynasty. In the Stele, Khufu himself tells of his discoveries made while clearing away the sands from the Pyramid and Sphinx. He dedicated the account to Isis, who he called the "Mistress of the Western Mountain," "Mistress of the Pyramid," and identified the Pyramid itself as the "House of Isis."

The Stele describes how Pharaoh Khufu, "gave to her (Isis) an offering anew, and he built again (to restore, renovate, reconstruct) her temple of stone." From there, the Pharaoh inspected the Sphinx, according to the text, and related the story of how in his time both the monument and a nearby sycamore tree had been struck by lightning. The bolt had knocked off part of the headdress of the Sphinx, which Khufu carefully restored. Egyptologist Selim Hassan, who dug out the Sphinx from the surrounding sands in the 1930s, observed there is indeed evidence that portions of the Sphinx were damaged by lightning, and the mark of ancient repairs is very apparent. Also, he noted, sycamore trees once grew to the south of the monument, which had been dated to a great age.

The Stele then ends with the story of how Khufu built small pyramids for himself and his daughters, wife and family, next to the Great Pyramid. Today, the ruins of three small pyramids are indeed situated on the east side of the monument. Archaeologists have found independent evidence that the southernmost of the three small pyramids flanking the Great Pyramid was in fact dedicated to Henutsen, a wife of Khufu. Everything in the inscription thus matches the known facts. If these facts can be believed as true, then the additional information that Khufu was only a restorer of the Great Pyramid and not its builder, must also be treated as historically true.

Ancient Legends & Modern Research Confirm Each Other

When we look at mythic history for the story of the origins of the Great Pyramid, we discover that the monument was not attributed to any pharaoh, but was the product of the genius and higher learning of the Gods of Old. Time and time again, from the Roman Marcellinus to the Coptic Al Masudi and the Arab Ibn Abd Alhokim, the recounters of the ancient legends tell how the pyramid was built to preserve the knowledge of a magnificent civilization from destruction by a flood, and that it was this flood which brought the Age of the Gods to its tragic end. The various Chronologies of Legendary Rulers place a minimum date for the

Age of the Gods as circa 10,000 B.C. This is the time frame Plato, in his Timaeus and Critias, ascribed the destruction of Atlantis. And it is also this date, as can be proven in modern scientific studies, which was highlighted by major climatic, geologic and geomagnetic disturbances, accompanied by massive paleo-biological extinctions in the planet, marking the division point between the Ice Age and the Present Era.

In Egypt, geologists examining the fossil record have found that the combined effect of melting glaciers in the Mountains of the Moon, plus a sharp rise in precipitation levels in Central Africa, caused the Nile river circa 10,000 B.C. to swell in size a thousandfold, eroding away cliff walls miles from its present banks, and washing out its entire valley throughout the length of Egypt. At the same time, as the Mediterranean Sea began to fill and rise due to higher ocean levels from melting northern glaciers, its waters for a brief period also flooded the lower Nile valley. These, geologists are certain, are the last major flood events in Egypt's fossil history, before the sea retreated and the Nile settled down to today's relatively peaceful, winding flow. Yet, knowing this, geologists are hard pressed to explain why there existed a four-teen-foot layer of silt sediment around the base of the Pyramid, a layer which also contained many seashells, and the fossil of a sea cow, all of which were dated by radiocarbon methods to 11,600 B.P. (Before Present) plus or minus 300 years.

Legends and records likewise speak of the fact that, before the Arabs removed the pyramid's outer casing stones, one could see water marks on the stones halfway up the pyramid's height, in about the 240-foot level, which would be 400 feet above the present Nile level. The medieval Arab historian Al Biruni, writing in his treatise *The Chronology of Ancient Nations,* noted: "The Persians and the great mass of Magians relate that the inhabitants of the west, when they were warned by their sages, constructed buildings of the King and the Giza Pyramids. The traces of the water of the Deluge and the effects of the waves are still visible on these pyramids halfway up, above which the water did not rise." Add to this the observation made when the pyramid was first opened, that incrustations of salt an inch thick were found inside. Most of this salt is natural exudation from the chambered rock wall, but chemical analysis also shows some of the salt has a mineral content consistent with salt from the sea. Thus, during the prehistoric Flood, when waters surrounded the Great Pyramid, the known and unknown entrances leaked, allowing seawater into the interior, which later evaporated and left the salts behind. The locations where the salts are found are consistent with the monument having been submerged half-way up its height.

If the floodings of 10,000 B.C. were the last major catastrophic water events in Egypt, and the pyramid exhibits signs of having been subjected to them, it means the pyramid must date from a period before the flooding occurred.

Though most Egyptologists today have yet to accept such a necessary "radical" revision of their dating of the pyramid, there have been other discoveries that have forced them to at least realize that their preconceived theories of any early Dynastic age for the structure is no longer tenable.

In 1983 and 1984, prehistorian Robert J. Wenke from the University of Washington, and president of the American Research Center in Egypt, was given permission to collect mortar samples from various ancient construction sites, including the Great Pyramid and the Sphinx Temple. The mortar contained particles of charcoal, insect matter, pollen, and other organic materials which could be subjected for carbon-14 dating analysis. Using two different radiocarbon dating laboratories—the Institute for the Study of Man at Southern Methodist University, and the Institute of Medium Energy Physics in Zurich—the samples revealed a number of curiosities. For the Great Pyramid samples, the tests performed at the two labs initially gave very different clusterings of dates, off by several thousands of years. When certain "adjustments" in the data were applied, the resulting time frame narrowed to 3100 B.C. to 2850 B.C.—which is still 400 years earlier than when most Egyptologists believe the Great Pyramid was built. Even more anomalous, the dates obtained from mortar used near the top of the Pyramid were a thousand years older than those obtained from mortar nearer the Pyramid base. The researchers, if they were to fully believe these findings, would have to propose that the pyramid had somehow been built from the top down.

What makes the datings further unacceptable is that all of them were taken from areas of previously exposed surfaces. We know from such sources as the Inventory Stele that the Giza monuments were time and time again subjected to many reconstructions and repair work, inside and out. Therefore the radiocarbon dates can only give us clues as to when the time frame was for the repair work, not the actual construction of the Great Pyramid. If the dates are to be believed at all, they at least tell us that reconstruction work was done on the monument in a time period long before the "accepted" building was done, which means the Pyramid itself must be from an even earlier period, farther distant in the past.

Were the Three Giza Pyramids Models for Egypt's "Pyramid Age"?

Expanding our sphere of inquiry to now include all three of the Giza Pyramids, we find that an interesting historical conundrum arises regarding their "accepted" construction. If, as conservative scholars surmise, the three Giza Pyramids were built in the Fourth Dynasty by the succession of three Pharaohs—Khufu, Khafre and Menkhare—what we find regarding the sizes of the three pyramids in association with the three reigns is inconsistent with what we would have expected to have happened.

First, Khufu ruled and supposedly constructed the Great Pyramid. Khafre followed Khufu, and in order to be politically and religiously "correct," we would have expected him to have erected a pyramid larger than Khufu's. To do otherwise would have seriously reflected on his being inferior to his predecessor. Generally speaking, a ruler could not afford for his people to think that their pharaoh was weaker in power and less blessed by the gods and goddesses than the ruler before him.

After Khafre, Menkhare next took the throne of Egypt, and in order to be in continued good political and religious form, we would have expected him to build the largest pyramid of all, dwarfing those of Khufu and Khafre in order to make sure he was not to be outshone by either of his predecessors.

Yet what we find at Giza is exactly opposite the expected scenario: Supposedly Khufu constructed the largest pyramid, Khafre built his slightly smaller than Khufu's, and Menkhare erected a pyramid only a third the size of the other two.

If what actually happened contradicts what should have happened if the three Giza pyramids were built in the Fourth Dynasty, then this can only mean that something is fundamentally wrong with the accepted scenario.

Instead of the three pharaohs building the three Giza pyramids, what if the pyramids were already present, old with age, and in the Fourth Dynasty the three succeeding rulers simply claimed possession of the structures, doing repair work on them, and building only the minor subsidiary pyramids around them for themselves and their families—just as the Inventory Stele describes Khufu did. What would we expect would have happened?

Khufu, first on the scene, would naturally have laid claim to the largest pyramid for himself, or the Great Pyramid. His successor, Khafre, now left with only two pyramids to choose from, would have taken possession of the second largest. Menkhare, the last to reign, would have had to be content with the last pyramid available, the smallest of the three.

Such a scenario best fits the actual facts, for this is exactly the succession of pyramids the pharaoh had jurisdiction over, each in their turn. Clearly, what this suggests is the Giza pyramids came first, then the pharaohs ruled, not the other way around.

According to conservative scholars, the Giza Three were supposed to represent the "height of accomplishment" in the Egyptian age of pyramid building, from the Third to the Thirteenth Dynasties, 2700 to 1800 B.C. But if the Giza Pyramids are in reality 12,000 years old, then they instead must have served as the models the Dynastic Egyptians repeatedly tried to copy and emulate. If we recognize this greater antiquity for the Giza Three, then many mysteries surrounding the design and construction of Egypt's other pyramids find their solutions.

The conservative view purports that the early pyramids along the Nile developed by stages of "evolution." Initially, in the First and Second Dynasties, from circa 3200 to 2800 B.C., the pharaohs were buried in mastabas, which were rectangular-shaped structures with walls sloping inward, built over underground vaults. What has baffled archaeologists is that each of the first kings of Egypt had not one but two such mastabas, at Abydos, and at Saqqara. One of these served as a cenotaph, or an empty tomb in honor of the royal person. The reason for this early practice is still a puzzle to scholars, not yet solved.

However, we know from ancient records that the peoples of the ancient world at one time had knowledge of the existence of the known entrance to the Great Pyramid, and they left evidence, in the form of torch soot and graffiti on the walls, that they penetrated as far as the Descending Passage and Pit Chamber. The Second and Third Pyramids also possess passages and empty chambers deep beneath their foundations. Did the early pharaohs, in studying the design of the Giza Pyramids standing silently before them on the Nile, imitate the empty pyramid chambers in the building of their second royal tombs, believing the empty chambers had a special spiritual significance they wished to emulate?

In the Third Dynasty, beginning about 2780 B.C., Pharaoh Zoser undertook to build a mastaba for himself as had his predecessors, but then decided to go several steps further. Two more mastaba structures were constructed on top of the first in step fashion, and finally, these in turn were incorporated as one side of a six-tiered pyramid. The development of this curious structure—today called the Step Pyramid, and located at Saqqara— indicates that Zoser was attempting to copy or duplicate a particular image. The pyramid does resemble a Sumerian ziggurat, or "holy mountain," except that unlike the ziggurat Zoser's structure possessed no sanctuary at its apex, and had a system of internal tunnels and chambers. The only structures which come close to being models for Zoser's work are the Giza Pyramids.

Significantly—and again in imitation of the Giza monuments— Zoser was not buried in his Step Pyramid. The foot of a mummy thought to have belonged to Zoser was found in one chamber, but the wrappings proved to be from a period much later than the Third Dynasty. All in all, a total of sixty mummies were found in and around the Step Pyramid, but these have been dated to the Saitic or Late Period, in the first millennium B.C. Zoser's tomb has been identified as located at Bet Khalaif, and no pyramid structure was found associated with it.

Following Zoser, his successor, Pharaoh Sekhemket, attempted to build a pyramid, but it appears never to have been completed, and today is only a mass of rubble. However, archaeologists did find at the bottom of a shaft below the structure a sealed alabaster sarcophagus. When the sarcophagus was opened, it was found to be completely empty, mirroring the state the Stone Box was found in, in the Great Pyramid.

The one ruler who by far was the most ambitious pyramid builder of the Third Dynasty was Pharaoh Senefru. He constructed three monuments, and there is every reason to believe he attempted to duplicate the feat of the three Giza Pyramids. He came close, for his pyramids contained two-thirds as much stone, covered 90 percent as much area, and were built with comparable speed as the Giza structures. The one obvious difference is their building design and masonry were very crude, when examined alongside the work done in the Giza area.

It is in the period immediately following Senefru, at the beginning of the Fourth Dynasty, that we are supposed to believe that Egyptian architects somehow miraculously overcame all their construction shortcomings, and developed the quantum leap of techniques for advanced building that went into the making of the Giza Pyramids. But the Giza monuments, however, stand out above all the rest of the pyramids in Egypt in many unique ways, clearly showing they were not related to the other Egyptian pyramids in time or construction.

First, only the Great Pyramid and (from what is known from legend and esoteric literature) the other two Giza Pyramids have chambers in their upper interior—all the rest possess only a lower chamber or chambers near the foundation. These are copies of the pit chambers in the Giza Pyramids. The Dynastic Egyptians, not knowing of the secret chambers higher up, had no precedent for including these in their own pyramids.

Second, only the Giza Three are accurately aligned to true north, which is indicative of a very sophisticated science of earth measurement and construction—elements exhibited in no other pyramid.

Third, only the Giza monuments were built with a high degree of accuracy—this precision, coupled with the apparent mastery of large, multi-ton stone construction, is what allowed the Giza Pyramids to reach their gigantic size, the largest in Egypt. In the Second and Third Pyramids the construction blocks are often not as massive or as finely positioned as they are seen in the

Great Pyramid, but they are precise enough to place them in an entirely different category from all other structures along the Nile.

Fourth, the Giza monuments were built using construction designs totally alien to any other pyramid form. As William R. Fix, in *Pyramid Odyssey* observed: "Because the other pyramids consist of much smaller blocks, they were built as a series of shells with multiple internal retaining walls to give cohesiveness. The three large Giza Pyramids do not have these internal casings. The very size of the blocks produces the necessary stability. This characteristic reveals a general excellence of workmanship and also imply a much higher technological capability than that employed anywhere else..

And fifth, unlike any pyramid supposedly built either before or after the Giza Three, none of the Giza monuments contain religious symbols or pictures in any of their inner chambers.

According to conservative scholars, the Giza Pyramids were built by the Fourth Dynasty Pharaohs Khufu, Khafre and Menkhare, as tombs. Yet not one of their bodies was found in any of them. The King's Chamber in the Great Pyramid was discovered to be completely empty upon its opening, its Stone Box sealed but vacant. In the Belzoni Chamber, beneath the Second Pyramid, a stone box was found like the one in the Great Pyramid, but it too contained no corpse. In 1878, a sarcophagus with a mummy inside was brought to light in the Third Pyramid. Though both the sarcophagus and mummy were lost at sea during their transport to the British Museum, samples had been taken from them, and when later analyzed by radiocarbon dating techniques, they were found to be from a fairly late date, only 2,000 to 2,500 years ago.

It is becoming increasingly apparent that the three pharaohs who are thought to have built the Giza Pyramids instead simply claimed the monuments as their own, having given up on the idea of attempting to duplicate the structures, as Senefru had tried but failed to do before them. There are several subsidiary pyramids around the Giza Three which were probably built by the pharaohs, and today are almost in total ruins because of their greatly inferior construction. According to ancient stelae and legends, the pharaohs also made repairs on the pyramids—but had nothing to do with their actual construction.

With Menkhare came the end of the Fourth Dynasty, and at the beginning of the Fifth Dynasty we are supposed to believe, according to the historians, that the Egyptians suddenly reverted back to the same old methods of design and greatly inferior construction techniques as seen in the pyramids prior to the Fourth Dynasty. The first pharaoh, Shepeskaf, actually built nothing more than a mastaba for his burial place. He was then followed by Userkaf, whose pyramid was so badly made it today is only a heap of debris. Sahure, Nieswerre and Neferirkare came next, and between them at Abu Sir they attempted to erect three pyramids (again duplicating Giza), but these in no way approached the size or grandeur of the Giza Three, and today are nothing more than broken piles. The same can be said for the monuments of the Sixth through the Thirteenth Dynasties, after which pyramid building for the most part came to an end. In all, 23 major pyramids were erected following the Fourth Dynasty and in each single case, the work on them was done hastily, with little care of precision, and using blocks that were no more than roughly squared boulders. We may well ask, if the Giza Pyramids, in all their excellence, were supposedly built in the Fourth Dynasty, what happened to the advanced knowledge seen in their design and construction—why was it never used again, in not a single later pyramid?

Author William R. Fix concluded: "The many fundamental differences between the major Giza monuments and the rest of Egypt's pyramids indicates that they do not fit into the contended chronology for dynastic Egypt. But if they do not belong to dynastic Egypt, there is only one direction in which they can be moved—not forward, but back into the past."

In truth, the Giza Pyramids were not an integral part of the evolutionary development of the Egyptian pyramids. Instead, they were there from the very beginning, the motivation and influence which spurred the building of the Dynastic pyramids along the Nile.

10
Egyptian Machining
by Christopher Dunn

Within the past three years, artifacts established as icons of ancient Egyptian study have developed a new aura. There are suggestions of controversy, coverups and conspiracy to squelch or ignore data that promises to shatter conventional academic thinking regarding prehistoric society. As of this writing, a powerful movement is intent on restoring to the world a heritage that has been partly destroyed and undeniably misunderstood. This movement consists of specialists in various fields who, in the face of fierce opposition from Egyptologists, are cooperating with each other to affect changes in our beliefs of prehistory.

The opposition by Egyptologists is like the last gasp of a dying man. In the face of expert analysis they are striving to protect their cozy tenures by arguing engineering subtleties that make no sense whatever. In a recent interview, an Egyptologist ridiculed theorists who present different view of the pyramids, claiming their ideas are the product of overactive imaginations stimulated by the consumption of beer. Hmmm.

By way of challenging such conventional theories, there has been, for decades, an undercurrent of speculation that the pyramid builders were highly advanced in their technology. Attempts to build pyramids using the orthodox methods theorized for the

Reprinted from Atlantis Rising Magazine, issue #8.

ancient Egyptians, have fallen pitifully short. The Great Pyramid is 483 feet high and houses seventy-ton pieces of granite lifted to a level of 175 feet. Theorists have struggled with stones weighing up to two tons to a height of a few feet. One wonders if these were attempts to prove that primitive methods are capable of building the Egyptian pyramids or the opposite? Attempts to execute such conventional theories have not revealed the theories to be correct! Do we need to revise the theory, or will we continue to educate our young with erroneous data?

In August 1984 this author published an article in *Analog Magazine* entitled "Advanced Machining in Ancient Egypt?" based on *Pyramids and Temple of Gizeh*, by Sir William Flinders Petrie, published in 1883. Since that article's publication, I have been fortunate to visit Egypt twice. With each visit I leave with more respect for the industry of the ancient pyramid builders. An industry, by the way, that does not exist anywhere in the world today.

In 1986, I visited the Cairo museum and gave a copy of my article, and a business card, to the director. He thanked me kindly, then threw my offering into a drawer with other sundry stuff, and turned away. Another Egyptologist led me to the "tool room" to educate me in the methods of the ancient masons by showing me a few cases that housed primitive copper tools.

I asked my host about the cutting of granite, as this was the focus of my article. He explained how a slot was cut in the granite and wooden wedges, soaked with water, were inserted. The wood swelled creating pressure that split the rock. This still did not explain how copper implements were able to cut granite, but he was so enthusiastic with his dissertation, I chose not to interrupt.

I was musing over a statement made by Egyptologist Dr. I. E. S. Edwards in "Ancient Egypt" (National Geographic Society, Washington, 1978). Edwards said that to cut the granite, "axes and chisels were made of copper hardened by hammering."

This is like saying "to cut this aluminum saucepan they fashioned their knives out of butter!"

My host animatedly walked me over to a nearby travel agent encouraging me to buy plane tickets to Aswan, "where" he said, "the evidence is clear. I must see the quarry marks there and the unfinished obelisk." Dutifully, I bought the tickets and arrived at Aswan the next day.

The Aswan quarries were educational. The obelisk weighs approximately 3,000 tons. However, the quarry marks I saw there did not satisfy me as being the only means by which the pyramid builders quarried their rock. Located in the channel, which runs the length of the obelisk, is a large hole drilled into the bedrock hillside, measuring approximately 12 inches in diameter and three feet deep. The hole was drilled at an angle with the top intruding into the channel space. (see photo) The ancients must have used drills to remove material from the perimeter of the obelisk, knocked out the webs between the holes and then removed the cusps.

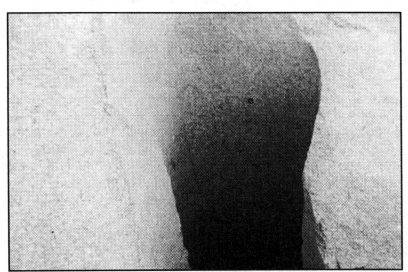

Evidence of the pyramid builders' true quarrying methods. A large hole drilled in the bedrock near the unfinished obelisk at the Aswan Quarries.

While strolling around the Giza Plateau later, I started to question the quarry marks at Aswan even more. (I also questioned why the Egyptologist had deemed it necessary to buy a plane ticket to look at them.) I was to the South of the second pyramid when I found an abundance of quarry marks of similar nature. The granite casing stones, which had sheathed the second pyramid, were stripped off and lying around the base in various stages of destruction. Typical to all of the granite stones worked on were the same quarry marks that I had seen at Aswan earlier in the week.

This discovery confirmed my suspicion of the validity of Egyptologists' theories on the ancient pyramid builders' quarrying methods. If these quarry marks distinctively identify the people who created the pyramids, why would they engage in such a tremendous amount of extremely difficult work only to destroy their work after having completed it? It seems to me that these kinds of quarry marks were from a later period of time and were created by people who were interested only in obtaining granite, without caring from where they got it.

You can see demonstrations of primitive stone cutting in Egypt if you go to Saqqara. Being alerted to the presence of tourists, workers will start chipping away at limestone blocks. It doesn't surprise me that they choose limestone for their demonstration, for it is a soft sedimentary rock and can be easily worked. However, you won't find any workers plowing through granite, an extremely hard, igneous rock made up of feldspar and quartz. Any attempt at creating granite, diorite and basalt artifacts on the same scale as the ancients, but using primitive methods, would meet with utter and complete failure.

Those Egyptologists who know that work-hardened copper will not cut granite have dreamed up a different method. They propose that the ancients used small round diorite balls (another extremely hard igneous rock) with which they "bashed" the granite.

How could anyone who has been to Egypt and seen the wonderful intricately detailed hieroglyphs cut with amazing precision in granite and diorite statues, that tower 15 feet above an average man, propose that this work was done by bashing the granite with a round ball? The hieroglyphs are amazingly precise with grooves that are square and deeper than they are wide. They follow precise contours and some have grooves that run parallel to each other with only .030-inch wide wall between the grooves. Sir William Flinders Petrie remarked that the grooves could only have been cut with a special tool that was capable of plowing cleanly through the granite without splintering the rock. Bashing with small balls never entered Petrie's mind. But then, Petrie was a surveyor whose father was an engineer. Failing to come up with a method that would satisfy the evidence, Petrie had to leave the subject open.

We would be hard pressed to produce many of these artifacts today, even using our advanced methods of manufacturing. The tools displayed as instruments for the creation of these incredible artifacts are physically incapable of even coming close to reproducing many of the artifacts in question. Along with the enormous task of quarrying, cutting and erecting the Great Pyramid and its neighbors, thousands of tons of hard igneous rock, such as granite and diorite, were carved with extreme proficiency and accuracy. After standing in awe before these engineering marvels and then being shown a paltry collection of copper implements in the tool case at the Cairo Museum, one comes away with a sense of frustration, futility and wonder.

Evidence of high-tech machining in Ancient Egypt. A 3-dimensional contoured block of granite which displays astounding accuracy and repeatability.

The world's first Egyptologist, Sir William Flinders Petrie, recognized that these tools were insufficient. He admitted it in his book *Pyramids and Temples of Gizeh* and expressed amazement and stupefaction regarding the methods the ancient Egyptians were using to cut hard igneous rocks, crediting them with methods that "...we are only now coming to understand." So why do modern Egyptologists identify this work with a few primitive copper instruments and small round balls? It makes no sense whatsoever!

While browsing through the Cairo Museum, I found evidence of lathe turning on a large scale. A sarcophagus lid had distinctive indications. Its radius terminated with a blend radius at shoulders on both ends. The tool marks near these corner radii are the same as those I have witnessed on objects that have an intermittent cut.

Petrie also studied the sawing methods of the pyramid builders. He concluded that their saws must have been at least nine feet long. Again, there are subtle indications on the artifacts Petrie was studying of modern sawing methods. The sarcophagus in the King's Chamber inside the Great Pyramid has saw marks on the north end that are identical to saw marks I've seen on modern granite artifacts.

The artifacts representing tubular drilling, studied by Petrie, are the most clearly astounding and conclusive evidence yet presented to identify, with little doubt, the knowledge and technology in existence in pre-history. The ancient pyramid builders used a technique for drilling holes that is commonly known as "trepanning." This technique leaves a central core and is an efficient means of hole making. For holes that didn't go all the way through the material, the craftsmen would reach a desired depth and then break the core out of the hole. It was not just the holes that Petrie was studying, but the cores cast aside by the masons who had done some trepanning. Regarding tool marks which left a spiral groove on a core taken out of a hole drilled into a piece of granite, he wrote: "the spiral of the cut sinks .100 inch in the circumference of six inches, or one in sixty, a rate of plowing out of the quartz and feldspar which is astonishing."

For drilling these holes, there is only one method that satisfies the evidence. Without any thought to the time in history when these artifacts were produced, analysis of the evidence clearly points to ultrasonic machining. This is the method that I proposed in my article in 1984, and so far, no one has been able to disprove it.

In 1994 I sent a copy of the article to Robert Bauval (*The Orion Mystery*) who then passed it on to Graham Hancock (*Fingerprints of the Gods*). After a series of conversations with Hancock, I was invited to Egypt to participate in a documentary with him, Robert and John Anthony West. On February 22, 1995 at 9:00 A.M. I had my first experience of being 'on camera'.

This time, with the expressed intent of inspecting features I had identified on my previous trip in 1986, I took some tools with me: a flat ground piece of steel (commonly known as a "parallel" in tool shops, it is about six inches long and a quarter-inch thick with edges ground flat within .0002 inch); an Interapid indicator; a wire contour gauge; a device which forms around shapes; and hard forming wax.

While there, I came across, and was able to measure, some artifacts produced by the ancient pyramid builders that prove beyond a shadow of a doubt that highly advanced and sophisticated tools and methods were employed. The first object I checked for close precision was the sarcophagus inside the second (Khafra's) pyramid on the Giza Plateau. I climbed inside the box, and with a flashlight and the parallel, was astounded to find the surface on the inside of the box perfectly smooth and perfectly flat. Placing the edge of the parallel against the surface I lit my flashlight behind it. There was no light coming through the interface. No matter where I moved the parallel, vertically, horizontally, sliding it along as one would a gauge on a precision surface plate, I couldn't detect any deviation from a perfectly flat surface. A group of Spanish tourists found it extremely interesting too, and gathered around me as I was becoming quite animated at this point exclaiming into my tape recorder. "Space-age precision!"

The tour guides, at this point, were becoming quite animated too. I sensed that they probably didn't think it was appropriate for a live foreigner to be where they believe a dead Egyptian should go, so I respectfully removed myself from the sarcophagus and continued my examination on the outside. There were more features of this artifact that I wanted to inspect, of course, but didn't have the freedom to do so.

My mind was racing as I lowered my frame into the narrow confines of the entrance shaft and climbed to the outside. The inside of a huge granite box finished off to a precision that we reserve for precision surface plates? How did they do this? It would be impossible to do this by hand!

While being extremely impressed with this artifact, I was even more impressed with other artifacts found at another site in the rock tunnels at the temple of Serapeum at Saqqara, the site of the step pyramid and Zoser's tomb. In these dark, dusty tunnels are housed 21 huge basalt boxes. They weigh an estimated 65 tons each and are finished off to the same precision as the sarcophagus in the second pyramid.

The final artifact I inspected was a piece of granite I quite literally stumbled across while strolling around the Giza Plateau later that day. I concluded, after doing a preliminary check of this piece, that the ancient pyramid builders had to have used a machinery that followed precise contours in three axes to guide the tool that created it. Beyond the incredible precision, normal flat surfaces, being simple geometry, may be explained away by simple methods. This piece, though, drives us beyond the question normally pondered...what tools were used to cut it? To a more far reaching question...what guided the cutting tool? These discoveries have more implications for understanding the technology used by the ancient pyramid builders than anything heretofore uncovered.

The interpretation of these artifacts depends on engineers and technologists. When presenting this material to a local engineers club, I was gratified by the response of my peers. They saw the significance. They agreed with the conclusions. While my focus was on the methods used to produce them, some engineers, ignoring Egyptologists' proposed uses for these artifacts, asked, "what were they doing with them?" They were utterly and completely astounded by what they saw.

The interpretation and understanding of a civilizations' level of technology cannot and should not hinge on the preservation of a written record for every technique that they had developed. The "nuts and bolts" of our society do not always make good copy, and a stone mural will more than likely be cut to convey an ideological message, rather than the technique used to inscribe it. Records of the technology developed by our modern civilization rest in media that is vulnerable and could conceivably cease to exist in the event of a worldwide catastrophe, such as a nuclear war, or another ice age. Consequently, after several thousand years, an interpretation of an artisan's methods may be more accurate than an interpretation of his language. The language of science and technology doesn't have the same freedom as speech. So even though the tools and machines have not survived the thousands of years since their use, we have to assume, by objective analysis of the evidence, that they did exist.

Christopher Dunn has worked in manufacturing for 35 years as a machinist, toolmaker and engineer. His analysis of the machining capabilities of the ancient Egyptians was featured in Graham Hancock's "Fingerprints of the Gods."

11

Beyond Giza
by John Anthony West

A s the new-millennium approaches, and with it, the shift into the next precessional 'age' of Aquarius, the enigmatic importance accorded that precessional shift by ancient cultures becomes a prominent feature of leading-edge scholarly research.

It is now apparent that knowledge of the precession did not begin with the Greeks–who have been credited with this discovery, as they have with just about everything that has led to contemporary science. (To fully appreciate the extent of the Eurocentric, white-supremacist con job foisted upon us as 'ancient history,' see Black Athena: The Afro-Asiatic Roots of Greek Civilization by Cornell Professor, Martin Bernal.)

But to complicate matters for Western scholars, prejudiced against a high pre-Greek science to begin with, knowledge of the precession was never referred to directly by the ancients. Rather, it was encoded into ancient myths, which often become comprehensible only when this astronomical element is discovered and acknowledged. At other times astronomical alignments based upon precessional phenomena determine the amazingly precise orientation of ancient temples, pyramids and whole cities.

From this body of new scholarship, two important aspects of precession emerge. The first is that this knowledge existed in re-

Reprinted from Atlantis Rising Magazine, issue #7.

motest antiquity, at times when there was not supposed to be any science at all, much less a sophisticated observational astronomy. This, in and of itself obliges a total re-think of the abilities of preliterate civilization and, with it, the supposed 'evolution' of human civilization. Secondly, as we acquire a new respect—indeed, a sense of wonder, if we have our emotional and intellectual faculties functioning—for the accomplishments of these vanished cultures, the question arises: What could it have been about this almost imperceptible cycle of the heavens that should so have entranced and preoccupied these very ancient cultures?

Or to put it another way: these civilizations were capable of technological feats whose methodology totally eludes the best scientific/engineering minds of today, yet an obdurate academic Establishment goes on insisting that slaves and ramps are enough to account for these marvels. Modern experts in building techniques assure us that slaves and ramps could not have constructed these edifices, and that advanced mathematical, geodesic and astronomical knowledge was absolutely required to account for the precision of their siting and their astounding earth-commensurate measures. So if these civilizations had at their command a technology totally different in kind from our own, in certain respects superior to our own, and at present, effectively unimaginable to us, what else did they know that we do not know?

The precession of the equinoxes was an event of such immense importance to them that they constructed their myths around it and orchestrated their gigantic stone monuments in such a way as to embody and reflect it. Perhaps it would be in our own interests to know just what it was that made the precession so important to them.

This question takes on special relevance, since we are now on the cusp of a precessional shift of particular potential importance. The ingress into Aquarius is one-half cycle in time (12,960 years) from the ingress into Leo, the period that (according to the work of the Flem-Ath's, Graham Hancock, Robert Bauval, ourselves and others) corresponds to the violent, sudden demise of that earlier high civilization. It was a span of a couple of thousand years of prodigious upheaval that it saw the sudden, violent disappearance of dozens of species of massive mammals all over the world, the final meltdown of the last Ice Age, a 300-foot rise in the world sea levels, and more or less coevally, (apparently) the construction of the Great Sphinx and in all likelihood the first structures on the Giza Plateau, and the mystery cities of the high Andes.

Thus the ingress into Leo marked a time of immense global change. To the rationalist mentality of modern-day science, this coincidence would be ascribed to just that: 'coincidence'. To the rationalist mentality, everything that cannot be explained is chalked up to 'coincidence', including, of course, the entire universe—the biggest 'coincidence' of all. To modern astronomers, precession is an astronomical event that takes place light years from earth, and is thereby devoid of influence or significance. However, for the advanced civilization that apparently prevailed on earth before and around that time, the fact of precession dominated its consciousness.

It is now becoming clear that somehow or another (the manner of transmission is by no means clear!) this sense of importance was passed down over seven millennia, to resurface in the mythology and in the monuments of the great civilizations of Egypt, Sumer, India and Mesoamerica.

Because so much remains of ancient Egypt, and it is so easily accessible, Egypt provides the richest field for contemporary study of this great precessional conundrum, along with the many other scientific and metaphysical mysteries of the distant past.

And, as though on cue, it is Egypt, above all other ancient cultures, that presently captures the imagination of the public. Tourists flock there, television shows (including our own) devoted to frontier research in alternative Egyptology draw huge audiences, and books on the subject become bestsellers. I am constantly receiving letters from grade school and high school teachers, telling me that on their own initiative, they have incorporated our work on the sphinx into their classes. Any new discovery in Egypt, even if inconsequential (e.g., the vastly over-ballyhooed K5, tomb of the sons of the Rameses the Great – which, unless something unplundered turns up in the excavation, will provide us with little we did not know before) makes front page newspaper news and provokes long articles in mainstream magazines. Ancient Egypt has moved into the forefront of the mass consciousness of the world.

As all of this unorthodox scholarship and, with it, 'Millennium Fever' captures the hearts and minds of the world, the academic Establishment itself remains obdurately opposed to it. Yet, unwittingly, it takes measures to feed the very fever it disparages...as though on cue.

Several significant sites—closed to the public for years—have recently been reopened or will soon reopen (some with restricted, expensive access, but open nonetheless). Each of these sites plays a role in the ongoing research and/or profoundly enhances our wonder and appreciation of Egypt as the site of a great and coherent Sacred Science.

The Great Pyramid

It is now possible for groups to 'rent' the Great Pyramid (or the nearby Khafre and Menkaure pyramids) for two hours prior to opening time or after closing time for a meditation session and/or detailed untroubled exploration of the pyramid's mysterious passageways and chambers. Not many people can spend two hours in the total resonant silence and impenetrable dark of the King's chamber and emerge still convinced this edifice was constructed solely to bury an egotistic king.

The Pyramids of Dahshur

Both these huge structures, The 'Bent' Pyramid and the 'Red' Pyramid, some twenty miles south of Giza, were built by Seneferu, father of Khufu (Cheops). The 'Bent' Pyramid incorporates—for reasons as yet undiscovered—two different angles of slope. The usual reason given is that the builders were starting off with an angle too steep for structural stability, and at the midway point were obliged to 'change their minds'. In Egyptology, structural anomalies are customarily ascribed to changes of mind by the 'primitive' builders of Egypt, even when these gigantic stone buildings themselves are built with the quite literal precision of a Swiss watch.

Structurally and stylistically the Dahshur pyramids are of a piece with the pyramids of Giza. I've long believed that these were part of one single, immense scheme, perhaps astronomical, but I hadn't a clue as to how to prove it. So, I'm pleased to note that in their groundbreaking forthcoming work on the Giza Plateau, The Message of the Sphinx, (due June 1996) Robert Bauval and Graham Hancock unriddle this particular great mystery in convincing fashion. They show that the Dahshur pyramids represent the two stars of the Hyades in a grand astronomical plan in which the Giza Pyramids are earthly reflections of the stars making up the belt of Orion. With the mighty Dahshur pyramids open to the public, visitors can now go try to capture, as best they can, the 'vibes' that the ancients went to such prodigious pains to provide.

Step Pyramid of Saqqara

The Step Pyramid

Built by King Zoser of the third Dynasty (ca 2700 B.C.), this is the first major pyramid built in Dynastic Egypt. And there is no mistaking that this is a tomb. Inscriptions say so. Huge stores of (nonprecious) funerary equipment were found there when it was first excavated. Unlike the pyramids of Giza and Dahshur, the internal chambers of the pyramid conform to common, standard Egyptian funerary architecture. Long closed for structural reasons, the pyramid will soon reopen. Though unquestionably dynastic Egyptian, the Zoser pyramid, and perhaps the entire complex, has demonstrable antecedents in that earlier epoch. Due east of the midpoint of the east face of the step pyramid, there is a deep shaft with tell-tale deeply water-weathered sides. This is a certain indication of an earlier date of origin. The shaft then connects to the face of the pyramid with a trough or perhaps an ancient passageway, filled in by blocks of stone. This strongly suggests that even the step pyramid is superimposed upon, or contains elements of, a still earlier construction.

The Tomb of Nefertari

Recently restored at great expense and with incredible care and attention by a team of Italian experts, this spectacularly beautiful tomb of the Great Queen of Rameses II can again be viewed (at a price of $30, and for limited numbers only each day). The original mineral pigments, cleaned of 3200 years of grime, now glow as fresh as the day they were painted. In ruins, Egypt is breathtaking; to see a bit of it, brought back into its original condition, is to experience Egypt as the Egyptian's themselves experienced it.

The Lighthouse of Alexandria

One of the original 'Seven Wonders of the World,' the fabled lighthouse was toppled into the sea by an earthquake in 1375 AD. It is in the process of underwater excavation, one of the most exciting finds of contemporary archeology. It once stood 640 feet high (roughly 60 stories—the Great Pyramid is 480 feet high) and its tower incorporated huge 75-ton blocks of granite that our biggest and best modern equipment cannot cope with. Egyptian authorities are debating how to handle this spectacular find. It may be turned into an underwater museum. Whatever its ultimate fate, it provides still another awe-inspiring example of the technology available to the ancients.

Travel to Egypt, a once-in-a-lifetime experience for just about everyone anyhow (excepting those bitten by the Egypt bug who return again and again, and—in the other camp—the emotionally defective and spiritually dyslexic, who just don't 'get' it) is now further enhanced for those able to take advantage of the opportunity provided by these recent reopenings and discoveries.

PART THREE
ANTARCTICA

12

When the Earth Moved
by J. Douglas Kenyon

In the not-too-distant future, Atlantis-seeking archeologists may have to trade in their sun hats and scuba gear for snow goggles and parkas.

If a rapidly growing body of opinion proves correct, instead of the bottom of the ocean, the next great arena of exploration for the fabled lost continent could be the frozen wastelands at the bottom of the earth. And before scoffing too vigorously, backers of North Atlantic, Aegean and other candidates would be well advised to give the new arguments for Atlantis in Antarctica a fair hearing.

Already enlisted in the ranks of those who take the notion very seriously are such luminaries as John Anthony West and Graham Hancock. Founded on a scientific theory developed by the late Dr. Charles Hapgood in close interaction with no less a personage than Albert Einstein, the idea appears robust enough to withstand the most virulent of attacks expected from the guardians of scientific orthodoxy. At any rate, it will not take a wholesale melting of the icecap to settle the question. A few properly directed satellite pictures and the appropriate seismic surveys could quickly make it clear if, indeed, advanced civilization has ever flourished on the lands beneath the ice.

Leading the charge of those betting that such evidence will

Reprinted from Atlantis Rising Magazine, issue #7.

soon be forthcoming are Canadian researchers Rand and Rose Flem-Ath, the authors of *When the Sky Fell*, just out in a new U.S. edition (St. Martin's Press, New York). Previously published in Canada, the book contains the couple's painstaking synthesis of Hapgood's theory of earth crust displacement and their own ground-breaking discoveries. The result has already won many converts. Graham Hancock believes the Flem-Aths have provided the first truly satisfactory answer to the question of just what happened to Plato's giant lost continent. Since devoting a chapter in his best-selling *Fingerprints of the Gods* to the work of the Flem-Aths, Hancock continues to opine in media appearances about the importance of their Antarctic theories. John Anthony West provides an afterword to the new edition of *When the Sky Fell* (Colin Wilson writes the introduction). Flem-Ath himself discussed his ideas on the February NBC Special, *The Mysterious Origins of Man*.

To get to the bottom of all the excitement, if not the planet, *Atlantis Rising* recently cornered Rand Flem-Ath at his home on Vancouver Island in British Columbia.

The author has not forgotten how his own interest in Atlantis began. In the summer of 1966, while waiting for an interview for a librarian's position in Victoria, British Columbia, he was working on a screenplay involving marooned aliens hibernating in ice on earth for 10,000 years. Suddenly, on the radio, came pop singer Donovan's hit "Hail Atlantis." "Hey, that's a good idea." he thought. "I wanted ice, so I thought, 'Now where can I have ice and an island continent?' and I thought of Antarctica."

Later, researching the idea, he read everything he could find on Atlantis, including Plato's famous account in *Criteas and Timeaus* where Egyptian priests described Atlantis, its features, location, history and demise to the Greek lawgiver Solon. At first the story didn't work for Flem-Ath, but that changed later when he made a startling discovery—unmistakable similarities between two obscure but remarkable maps.

A 1665 map by Jesuit scholar Athenasius Kircher, copied from much older sources, seemed to have placed Atlantis in the north Atlantic but strangely, had put north at the bottom of the page apparently forcing study upside down. The 1513 Piri Ri'is map, also copied from much more ancient sources, demonstrat-

Rand Flem-Ath / Photo by Mark Brett

ed that an ice-age civilization had sufficient geographic knowledge to accurately map Antarctica's coast as it existed beneath an ice cap many millennia old (as pointed out by Charles Hapgood in *Maps of the Ancient Sea Kings: Evidence of Advanced Civilization in the Ice Age*). What seemed obvious to Flem-Ath was that both maps depicted the same land mass.

Suddenly Antarctic Atlantis "stopped being a science fiction story." The revelation had dawned that it might be "something that could have been real." Further study of Plato yielded even more clues. "I noticed that the description is *from* Atlantis," he recalls. Soon, armed with a U.S. Navy map of the world, as seen from the South Pole, he discovered a new way of understanding Plato's story and a new way of looking at Kircher's map. Viewed from this southern perspective, all of the world's oceans appear as parts of one great ocean, or, as what is described in Plato as "the real ocean" and the lands beyond as a "whole opposite continent." Sitting in the middle of that great ocean, at the very navel of the world is Antarctica. Suddenly, it was possible to understand Kircher's map, as drawn, with north at the top, Africa and Madagascar to the left and the tip of South America on the right.

The term 'Atlantic Ocean,' Flem-Ath soon realized, had meant something quite different in Plato's time than it has since the age of exploration. To the ancients, it included all of the world's oceans. The idea becomes clearer when one remembers from Greek mythology that Atlas (a name closely related to Atlantis and Atlantic) held the entire world on his shoulders.

The "whole opposite continent," which surrounded the "real ocean" in Plato's account, consisted of South America, North America, Africa, Europe and Asia fused together in the Atlantean world view as though they were one continuous land mass. And in fact, these five continents were at the time (9,600 B.C.) one landmass in the geographic sense.

Flem-Ath would render Plato's account to read: "Long ago the World Ocean was navigated beyond the Straits of Gibraltar by sailors from an island larger than North Africa and the Middle East combined. After leaving Antarctica you would encounter the Antarctic archipelago (islands currently under ice) and from them you would reach the World Continent which encircles the World Ocean. The Mediterranean Sea is very small compared to the World Ocean and could even be called a bay. But beyond the Mediterranean Sea is a World Ocean which is encircled by one continuous landmass."

A common mistake in most readings of Plato, Flem-Ath believes, is the inappropriate attempt to interpret the ancient account in the light of modern concepts. Another example is the familiar reference to the "Pillars of Hercules," beyond which Atlantis was said to reside. While it is true that the term sometimes referred to the Straits of Gibraltar, another, equally valid interpretation is that it meant "the limits of the known world."

For Flem-Ath, the world as seen from Antarctica matched perfectly the ancient Egyptian's account of the world as seen from Atlantis. The ancient geography was in fact far more advanced than our own, which made sense if Atlantis was, as Plato argued, an advanced civilization.

Platonic theories notwithstanding, the most difficult challenge—explaining how Atlantis might have become Antarctica—remained. How could land, now covered with thousands of feet of ice, have once supported any kind of human habitation, to say nothing of a great civilization on the scale described by Plato? For the Flem-Aths, the answer, it turned out, had already been worked out—thoroughly, convincingly and published in the Yale Scientific Journal in the mid 1950s.

Dr. Charles Hapgood

In his theory of earth crust displacement, Professor Charles Hapgood had—citing vast climatalogical, paleontological, and anthropological evidence—argued that the entire outer shell of the earth, over its inner layers periodically shifts, bringing about major climatic changes. The climatic zones (polar, temperate and tropical) remain the same because the sun still shines from the same angle in the sky, but as the outer shell shifts, it moves through those zones. From the perspective of earth's population, it seems as though the sky is falling. In reality the earth's crust is shifting to another location. Some lands move toward the tropics. Others shift, with the same movement, toward the poles. While yet others escape great changes in latitude. The consequences of such a movement is, of course, catastrophic. Throughout the world, massive earthquakes shake the land and enormous tidal waves batter the continental shelves. As old ice caps forsake the polar zones, they melt, raising sea levels higher and higher. Everywhere, and by whatever means, people seek higher ground to avoid an ocean in upheaval.

The Flem-Aths corresponded with Hapgood from 1977 until his death in the early '80s and though he differed with them about the location of Atlantis (his candidate was the Rocks of Saint Peter and Saint Paul) he praised their scientific efforts to buttress his theory. In the summer of 1995, Flem-Ath was allowed to read Hapgood's voluminous correspondence (170 pages) with Albert Einstein and to discover a much more direct collaboration between the two than has been previously supposed.

Upon first hearing of the research—in correspondence from Hapgood—Einstein responded "very impressive...have the impression that your hypothesis is correct." Subsequently Einstein raised numerous questions which Hapgood answered with such thoroughness that Einstein was eventually persuaded to write a glowing foreword for Hapgood's book *Earth's Shifting Crust: A Key to Some Basic Problems of Earth Science* (1958 by Pantheon Books, New York).

Earth crust displacement is not mutually exclusive with the now widely accepted theory of continental drift. According to Flem-Ath "they share one assumption, that the outer crust is mobile in relation to the interior, but in plate tectonics the movement is extremely slow." Earth crust displacement suggests that over long periods of time, approximately 41,000 years, certain forces build toward a breaking point. Among the factors at work: a massive buildup of ice at the poles, distorting the weight of the crust; the tilt of the Earth's axis which changes by over three degrees every 41,000 years (not to be confused with the wobble which causes the precession of equinoxes); and the proximity of the Earth to the Sun which also varies over thousands of years.

"One of the common mistakes," says Flem-Ath, "is to think of the continents and the oceans as being separate, but really, the fact that there's water on certain parts of the plates is irrelevant. What we have in plate tectonics are a series of plates which are moving very gradually in relationship to each other. But what we have in earth crust displacement is all of the plates are considered as one single unit as part of the outer shell of the earth which changes place relative to the interior of the earth."

The theory, says Flem-Ath, offers elegant explanations for such phenomena as the rapid extinction of the Mammoths in Siberia, the near universal presence of cataclysmic myths among primitive people, and many geographic and geological anomalies left unexplained by any other theory. Most of the evidence usually cited to support the idea of ice ages serves earth crust displacement even better. Under the latter, some parts of the planet are always in an ice age when others are not. As lands change latitudes, they move either into or out of an ice age. The same change that put western Antarctica in the ice box also quickfroze Siberia but thawed out much of North America.

While many establishment geologists insist that the Antarctic ice cap is much older than the 11,600 years indicated by Plato, Flem-Ath points out that the core sampling on which most of the dating is based is taken from Greater Antarctica which was indeed under ice, even during the time of Atlantis. The suggestion here is that a movement of about 30 degrees or about 2,000 miles occurred within a relatively short span of time. Before

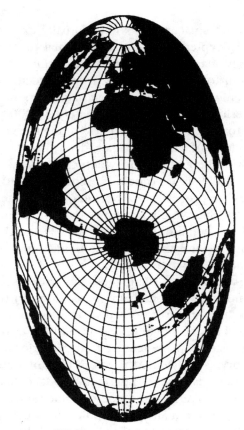

U.S. Navy map of the world

such a movement, the Palmer peninsula of Lesser Antarctica (the part closest to South America whose sovereignty is presently disputed by Chile, Argentina and Great Britain) would have projected an area the size of western Europe beyond the Antarctic circle into temperate latitudes reaching as far as Mediterranean-like climes. In the meantime Greater Antarctica would have remained under ice in the Antarctic circle.

"An area such as that described by Plato," says Flem-Ath "would be the size of Pennsylvania, with a city comparable to modern-day London." Not a bad target for satellite photography. Concentric circles or other large geometric features should be easily discernible through the ice.

Flem-Ath believes that in most areas, Plato should be taken at his word, though he does suspect that there may have been some fabrications in the story. The war between the Atlanteans and the Greeks, for example, he believes may have been cooked up to please the local audience. In regard to the scale of Atlantean achievement, however, he takes Plato quite seriously and is very impressed. "The engineering feats described," says Flem-Ath, "would have required incredible skill, moreso than even what we have today." As for the notion that Plato's numbers should be scaled down by a factor of ten—a frequent argument used to support claims that Atlantis was really the Minoan civilization in the Aegean—he doesn't buy it. "A factor of 10 error might be understandable when you are using Arabic numbers, with a difference between 100 and 1000 of one decimal place, but in Egyptian numbering, the difference between the two numbers is unmistakable." For him the argument is similar to the one for a North Atlantic location, in which a modern concept has been inappropriately superimposed upon an ancient one.

So far Flem-Ath's ideas have been largely ignored by the scientific establishment, but he believes that at least Hapgood's arguments may be getting close to some kind of acceptance. "Quite often new ideas take about 50 years to be absorbed," he says, "and we're getting close to the time."

If, in fact, satellite photography and seismic surveys produce the indications that Flem-Ath expects, what next? "The ice in the region that we are talking about is relatively shallow," he says, "less than half a kilometer, and once we've pinpointed the area, it should be relatively easy to sink a shaft and find something."

That 'something' could be among the finest and most dramatic artifacts ever discovered—quick-frozen and stored undisturbed for almost 12,000 years.

A prospect hot enough to melt the hearts of even the most hardened skeptics? We shall see.

PART FOUR
ANCESTORS FROM SPACE

13

Hollywood and the Star Gods
by Len Kasten

Coming events are said to cast their shadows. Some sci-fi mo-
viemakers seem to have a talent for tapping into that level
of the mass subconscious in which new concepts are in the for-
mative stages, and bringing them into public consciousness. Typically, their films are instantly very popular, often unexpectedly,
because the audiences, to the extent to which they also are in
touch with the subconscious, respond with interest and enthu-
siasm without consciously understanding why. Nothing is as inexorable as an idea whose time has come, and because film is
such a powerful medium, nothing can precipitate it as quickly as
a well-made movie that "opens wide." It is the "Hundreth Monkey" principle accelerated to warp speed! Consequently these
films usually become watershed events with permanent social effects. Stanley Kubrick's "2001—A Space Odyssey" and Steven
Spielberg's "Close Encounters of the Third Kind" are clearly in
this category. The "Star Trek" series has had such a profound social effect that it has actually evoked a sort of reverse nostalgia, a
longing for the "good new days!" And now, a possible new
"star" has appeared on the horizon.

MGM's recent film, "Stargate" has revived some of the old
excitement. As with the others, somehow this movie struck a
chord that resonated in the mass subconscious, and consequent-

Reprinted from Atlantis Rising Magazine, issue #3.

from MGM's Stargate

ly has enjoyed a surprising box office bonanza. The sequel is already in production. The movie's success would appear to validate growing public interest, and belief in, the concept of "ancient astronauts," a subject that has intrigued a small, but international, group of enthusiasts ever since the advent of Erich Von Daniken's book, "Chariots of the Gods," in 1968. "Star Wars" was the first popular film to address this milieu, claiming to have taken place "a long time ago, on a planet far away." Then, the popular TV series, "Battlestar Galactica" picked up on the theme, portraying the adventures of a band of nomadic stellar expatriates heading for the new promised land—Earth, eventually to become our ancestors.

In "Stargate," an ancient stone ring, about 30 feet in diameter, unearthed by archaeologists at Giza in Egypt in 1928, is discovered, in the present day, to be a "gate" to inter-stellar travel. When activated by a certain sequence of seven symbols, it permits travel through the gate. The Air Force takes over the project, and recruits an expert in hieroglyphics to decode the glyphs inscribed around the ring. He succeeds and they send through a probe and track its path all the way across the universe to a planet in another galaxy. A small Special Forces expedition is assembled. They go through the gate and find themselves in what appears to be an abandoned temple in the middle of a desert. Two tall obelisks stand at the entrance. A duplicate of the Great Pyramid of Giza stands nearby. While they know they are on a planet circling a distant star, the scene is very reminiscent of ancient Egypt. A huge spacecraft descends over the pyramid, and a youthful king, with his entourage, and bodyguards who resemble the Egyptian jackal-headed creatures, take residence in the temple. It is Ra, the Sun God—he who rides in the Celestial Disk. Ra keeps the people of a nearby city terrorized by means of high technology. He has winged craft equipped with death rays, and his bodyguards carry cylindrical ray guns. The people worship him as a god, and they are thus kept enslaved, working on mining operations. The story becomes predictable after this as the Earthlings, well acquainted with such problems, organize and lead the people and precipitate a revolution. The film is obviously suggesting that this is essentially what happened in ancient Egypt—that Ra and the other "gods" were extraterrestrial who made a profound impression on the predynastic Egyptians, who then memorialized a catalogue of religious rituals based on these early experiences. These rituals then eventually became solemn and sacred ceremonies carried out by the priests and pharaohs for thousands of years afterwards. According to at least one researcher, this scenario is uncannily close to the truth!

The Five Books of Zecharia

One of the foremost "ancient astronaut" theoreticians in the world today is Palestinian born Zecharia Sitchin. Sitchin is a walking Rosetta Stone—a multilingual scholar who acquired proficiency in ancient languages at an early age. He is the only investigator in this field in the world who reads ancient Sumerian, in addition to Hebrew, both ancient and modern, Greek and Aramaic, and who has developed high competency in Egyptian hieroglyphics. Sitchin has built a reputation for scrupulous and thorough scholarship and research, tempered with a healthy dose of intuition—a potent combination that gives his books an air of solid respectability and authority. Based primarily on his deciphering of thousands of Sumerian clay tablets, Sitchin has written a series of five books called *The Earth Chronicles* in which he lays out an elaborate story about space travelers from a theoretical 10th planet (12th if the Sun and Moon are included) in the solar system, about four times the size of Earth, called Nibiru, or Marduk in Babylonian.

Sitchin claims that this planet has a very eccentric orbit whereby it travels from way out beyond Pluto, cutting across the orbits of the rest of the planets, and then half-circling the Sun between Mars and Jupiter, taking 3,600 Earth years for each revolution. On its closest orbital approach, about 450,000 years ago, a band of Nibiruans known as the Anunnaki, came to Earth and landed in southern Mesopotamia. They then proceeded to mine gold, which they evidently needed for the survival of their planet. At first they extracted it from the Persian Gulf, but they couldn't obtain the quantities they needed that way, so they began underground mining in South Africa. The workers were not used to such backbreaking toil deep under the earth, and finally, after 40 Nibiru years, or 144,000 Earth years, they rebelled. This precipitated a visit to Earth by Anu, the Lord of Nibiru, and a meeting was convened to resolve the problem. It was decided to genetically engineer a race of slave workers by crossing the apelike creatures, then inhabiting Earth, with the Anunnaki. About 300,000 years ago, after a period of trial and error, they succeeded in achieving the "perfect model" of a primitive worker by implantation of the engineered embryo into the womb of a "birth goddess." Then they went into mass production. Using a group of fourteen goddesses, they produced seven humans of each gender at a time, and put them to work in the mines when they reached adulthood. At first they had to keep producing them because, as hybrids, they were sterile. But later, thanks to the experiments of Enki, the leader of the original expedition, they were able to develop a "model" that could reproduce. Initially, the "gods" were angry at Enki for giving humans this gift, but they eventually realized the advantages. Sitchin claims that this was the basis of the Adam and Eve story, and the advent of the human race. As humans proliferated, the Anunnaki put them to work on a variety of jobs including building their houses, or "temples."

Humans also cooked, danced and played music to entertain the gods. Such intimate fraternization ultimately led to the inevitable. The gods found the human females physically compatible and attractive and began to take them as wives. This explains the cryptic statement in Genesis, "the sons of god went in unto the daughters of men," which is now more understandable since the females were also descendants of the gods. This launched an era of Dionysian revelry by the gods, who acted much like drunken sailors in a foreign port, which their leaders found disturbing since it diluted their mission. Enlil, the Lord of the Earth, knew that the Antarctic ice cap would soon be plunged into the ocean because of Earth convulsions caused by the next approach of Nibiru. In order to end this orgy of miscegenation, it was decided to allow the human race to perish in the coming deluge while the Anunnaki orbited the Earth safely in their spacecraft. However, once again Enki came to the rescue of humanity, and secretly instructed the first human king, Ziusudra, in the construction of a submersible vessel. This, of course, is the Sumerian version of the story of Noah. The Advent of Ra.

Of Time and the Pyramids

There is now mounting evidence that the Giza pyramids are much older than the Fourth Dynasty, and that instead of having developed out of earlier primitive pyramids, they were actually the prototypes of the later pyramids, which were really pale imitations. They were clearly never used as tombs, and the technology displayed in their construction was much too advanced for the era of Khufu, about 2600 B.C., but very probably existed in "the time of the gods."

Sitchin points out that the most convincing piece of evidence that Khufu did not build the Giza monuments is the so-called "Inventory Stela" found in the Temple of Isis near the Great Pyramid. The inscription by Khufu makes reference to the pyramid and Sphinx as already standing. And in *The Stairway to Heaven* Sitchin makes a very convincing case for the fact that the red paint quarry marks referring to Khufu, discovered in 1837 in the sealed chambers over the King's Chamber, were forgeries. The Great Pyramid was built perfectly level and perfectly aligned with the four directions of the compass, with each side at a precise angle of 54 degrees. Says Sitchin, "The wonderment only increases as one realizes the interior complexities and preci-

sion of the galleries, corridors, chambers, shafts and openings...the locking and plugging systems...all in perfect alignment
with each other..." Consider what primitive equipment and tools
were available in that period. The Egyptians of that era did not
have knowledge of the pulley, or block and tackle. All they had
were wooden rollers and levers, and wood was at a premium in
the desert. Consider also the immense difficulty of transporting
those 2.3 million 200-ton stones from the quarry all the way
down the Nile at Aswan. If they cut, moved and placed ten
stones per day, it would have taken 632 years to completion.
The Great Pyramid still remains the largest stone structure in the
world, and probably could not be duplicated today. But for the
Anunnaki, it was probably not such a difficult feat. Ra's father,
Ptah or Enki, was known as an engineering genius, and Ra is said
to have enlisted the assistance of Thoth, the Egyptian god of sciences and of magical powers. This suggests that the Anunnaki
might have had the ability to move the massive stones around
without benefit of manpower.

The Pharaoh's Journey to the Stars

Robert Bauval, a construction engineer working in the Middle East, had always been fascinated by the sophisticated astronomical knowledge of the ancient Egyptians, and how it was incorporated into their religious ritual. As the god king, each
pharaoh was considered to be the personification of Horus, the
son of Osiris. According to the Pyramid Texts, the only authentic
source of information, the purpose of the whole process of
mummification and the accompanying rites was to prepare the
pharaoh for a journey to heaven in the stars, specifically Orion,
there to rejoin his father Osiris and to become a star in that constellation, as he was. To help in this journey, the priests would
frequently paint star maps on the insides of the coffin lids, or on
the ceilings of the tombs. "Live and be young beside your father,
beside Orion in the sky" says Pyramid Text 2180. About 1954, an
Egyptologist named Badawy advanced the theory that the shafts
in the Great Pyramid were not for ventilation at all, but were
pointed towards certain star systems, and had some religious significance. After making corrections for precession, he determined that around 2600 B.C., the time of Khufu, the southern

shaft pointed directly at the belt of Orion, making it very likely that some ritual was probably performed in the King's Chamber involving the flight of the soul of the pharaoh through the shaft to Orion. Bauval, who had always wondered why the three pyramids at Giza were aligned the way they were, was intrigued when he came across Badawy's data. He began to believe that there was some correlation between Orion and the building scheme at Giza. He pored over aerial photographs seeking some clue. Then, one night in November of 1983, on an overnight camping trip in the desert dunes near Riyadh, Saudi Arabia, he woke up around 3 A.M. and gazed at the stellar canopy above, so crystal clear he could almost touch it. He awoke his friend Jean-Pierre ̇and they observed and discussed the Milky Way, Orion and Sirius. Then Jean-Pierre pointed out how the third star in Orion's belt was smaller and slightly out of alignment with the other two. In ̇a flash Bauval realized that the three pyramids at Giza were a replication on Earth of the three stars in Orion's belt! He then perceived that the Orion stars were in approximately the same relation to the Milky Way, which resembles a great river in the sky, as the Giza pyramids were to the Nile. This was a momentous discovery, fraught with implications for both Egyptologists and ancient astronaut theorists alike. It indicated a grand plan at Giza far beyond the capability of Pharaoh Khufu. And if Ra was the builder of the pyramids, this would connect him with Orion in some way. Bauval's breakthrough is discussed in detail in his new book, *The Orion Mystery* (Crown, 1994) penned with co-author Adrian Gilbert. Bauval then went on to study precession, and discovered that Orion made its first appearance over the horizon at Giza in 10,400 B.C., almost exactly when Sitchin claimed that Ra had built the Giza pyramids! Sitchin never mentioned him (and Bauval never mentions Sitchin), but Bauval points out that famous clairvoyant Edgar Cayce also claimed that very same date to be the beginning of the design phase of the Great Pyramid. With a scientist/engineer, an anthropologist/linguist, and a clairvoyant adding their voices of concurrence, the case for the antiquity of the Giza pyramids and Sphinx seems impressive.

And so it appears that somehow "Stargate" has tapped into a vision of the distant past that no respectable anthropologist, archeologist or Egyptologist has ever painted, or would even dare to entertain. It has brought us the true story of Ra, the Star God— He of the Winged Globe. I guess if you want to learn the truth about the past, or to see into the future, you have to go to the movies. Pass the popcorn, please.

14

Visitors from Beyond
by J. Douglas Kenyon

From a Human Potentials conference in Washington, D.C. to a Whole Life Exposition in Seattle, from campus bull sessions in Berkeley to cocktail party discussions in Boston, no talk of the hot alternative explorations into the mysterious wellsprings of civilization gets very far these days without at least a passing reference to the work of Zecharia Sitchin. And there are no signs that interest in the author of the five volumes of *The Earth Chronicles*, and the forthcoming *Divine Encounters* from Avon Books, is cooling.

In fact, "Sitchinites," as his true-believers unabashedly call themselves, have managed to proclaim in nearly every available forum, from talk shows to the internet, their gospel according to Sitchin—namely that mankind owes most of its ancient legacy to visiting extraterrestrials. Moreover, Sitchinist 'evangelism' has—with some help from the movie *Stargate*—achieved a not insignificant foothold in the public imagination. And while many may quarrel with his conclusions, very few will dispute that the Russian-born Israeli resident and ancient language expert has indeed come up with some very intriguing, if not compelling, data.

Indeed, few can match Sitchin's scholarly credentials. One of a handful of linguists who can read Sumerian cuneiform text, he is also a recognized authority in ancient Hebrew as well as

Reprinted from Atlantis Rising Magazine, issue #5.

Egyptian hieroglyphics. Not a little controversy, though, surrounds his unusual method of interpreting the ancient texts. Whether Biblical, Sumerian, Egyptian or otherwise, Sitchin insists they should be read, not as myths, but quite literally, essentially as journalism. Forget about Jungian archetypes and metaphysical/spiritual analysis. "If somebody says a group of 50 splashed down in the Persian Gulf," he argues, "under the leadership of Enki and waded ashore and established a settlement, why should I say that this never happened, and this is a metaphor, and this is a myth, and this is imagination, and somebody just made it all up, and not say (instead) this tells us what happened."

Beginning with *The 12th Planet* in 1976, Sitchin has expanded his unique explanation of the ancient texts into a vast and detailed history of what he believes were the actual events surrounding mankind's origins. Presented is extensive 6,000-year-old evidence that there is one more planet in the solar system, from which "astronauts"—the biblical 'giants' (nephilim)—came to Earth in antiquity. Subsequent titles in *The Earth Chronicles* series were *The Stairway to Heaven* (1980), *The Wars of Gods and Men* (1985), *The Lost Realms* (1990) and *When Time Began* (1993). A companion book to the series *Genesis Revisited* was published in 1990. (For a summary, see the preceding chapter.)

Sitchin's describe in detail the evolving love/hate relationship between men and the 'gods' and how he believes that relationship shaped the early days of man on earth.

Whatever the Annunaki may have thought of their new creation, the literary critics have found Sitchin's work impressive. "A dazzling performance," raved the Kirkus Reviews. The Library Journal found it "Exciting...Credible."

Cornered recently at his New York office, the author took some time to comment for *Atlantis Rising* on his new book *Divine Encounters*—expected in stores in November just in time for the Christmas gift-buying season—and other topics of interest both modern and ancient.

Encounters relates many stories from Biblical, Sumerian and Egyptian sources. From the Garden of Eden to Gilgamesh, Sitchin believes all references to deity, or deities, are actually indicating the Annunaki, but he does distinguish between the current so-called UFO abduction experience as studied by Harvard professor John Mack and the ancient encounters. Stressing that he personally has never been abducted, he points out that whereas the current experience is usually viewed as a negative phenomenon with needles and other forms of unwelcome intrusion, "in ancient times, to join the deities was a great and unique privilege. Only a few were entitled to such an encounter."

Many of the encounters were sexual. The Bible "clearly states," he points out, "that they (the Anunnaki) 'chose as wives the daughters of men and had children by them, men of renown,' etc., the so-called demi-gods regarding which there are more explicit tales both in Mesopotamian literature and Egyptian so-called mythology, and Greek to some extent—Alexander the Great believed that these sons of the gods were mated with his mother." *The Epic of Gilgamesh* tells how one goddess tried to entice the hero into her bed and how that he suspected that if she succeeded he would end up dead. Other encounters involved "virtual reality," and experiences "akin to the Twilight Zone." Also up for an analysis are the experiences of the prophets Jeremiah, Ezekiel and Isaiah. Finally Sitchin claims to have unraveled the secret identity of the being named YHWH, and to have come to a "conclusion that is mind-boggling even for me." Nothing further could be elicited on the subject. "Buy the book," he suggests.

In the nearly 20 years since *The 12th Planet* first appeared, Sitchin has seen a considerable change in attitudes toward his work. Still, unlike von Dannikin and others, Sitchin's study has not been lambasted by other scientists, a fact which he attributes to the soundness of his research. "The only difference between me and the scientific community—I'm talking about Asyriologists, Sumeriaologists, etc.—is that they refer to all these texts which I read (literally) as mythology." Today, he says many researchers have come to follow his line of reasoning. By his latest reckoning, there are nearly thirty books by other writers which have "been spawned" by his writings.

While Sitchin's "facts" may be beyond challenge, many of his conclusions are another matter, even among today's most avant garde thinkers. Mars researcher Richard Hoagland complains that Sitchin is trying to "treat the Sumerian cuneiform text like some kind of ancient New York Times," while others, like symbolist scholar John Anthony West, believe subtleties in the high wisdom of the ancients have completely eluded Sitchin. For those, "his views are essentially simplistic and materialistic. He is a mechanistic reductionist and a throwback to 19th century positivism." Still others are reminded of the efforts of fundamentalist preachers to pin the mystical visions of Saint John the Revelator on specific historical personages (i.e., Napoleon or Hitler or Saddam Hussein as the anti-Christ, etc.).

Sitchin though remains unrepentant, with little use for what he calls "the established view," which he says "is that the texts deal with mythology and that it all is imagination, and—whether metaphor or not—that these things never happened. Someone just imagined them." In contrast, he has "no doubt that these things really happened."

The argument that the Sumerian and Egyptian civilizations got their impetus from extraterrestrials, however, does not rule out the notion that there could have been earlier and perhaps even more advanced civilizations on Earth. "There's no denial of that," he says, citing Sumerian and Assyrian writings. Ashurbanipal, for instance, said he could read writing from before the flood, and describes cities and civilizations that existed before the deluge, but which were wiped out by it. So on any question of whether there could have been an earlier civilization before the Sumerians or even before the flood—which Sitchin places at seven- to eight-thousand years prior, "the answer is absolutely yes." No matter how far back he goes, though, Sitchin sees only the hand of Annunaki behind human achievement.

Plato should be taken literally too, though Sitchin says he has some difficulty placing the location of Atlantis, "whether it was in the middle of the Atlantic Ocean, whether it was in the Pacific in what was known later as Mu or whether it was in Antarctica, I don't know what actually (Plato) was talking about, but the notion that once upon a time there was a civilization that was destroyed or came to an end through a major catastrophe, a great flood or something similar, I have absolutely no problem with that."

Sitchin is among those who believe the Great Pyramid is

Sitchin says the 'spacecraft' in the center is passing Mars on the right

much older than is maintained by orthodox Egyptology. In his second book *The Stairway to Heaven* he was at considerable pains to establish that the famous cartouche cited as evidence that the structure was built by Khufu, was, in fact, a forgery. Sitchin meticulously makes the case that Colonel Howard-Vyse actually faked the marks in the spaces above the King's Chamber where he claimed to have discovered them. Since publication, additional corroboration has come from the great grandson of the master mason who assisted Howard-Vyse. It seems that Colonel Vyse was seen entering the pyramid on the night in question with brush and paint pot in hand and was heard to state that he intended to reinforce some of the marks he had found, ostensibly to render them more legible. Upon failing to dissuade Howard-Vyse from his plan, the mason quit. The story, however, was kept alive and handed down through the family till it eventually came to Sitchin, further reinforcing his unshakable conviction of the true antiquity of the Great Pyramid.

Regarding the "face on Mars," Sitchin is more ambivalent.

to Earth on the left.

Whether or not the "face" is real or a product of light and sand, he is more impressed by other photographed structures. Citing his own training at Jerusalem's Hebrew university in the 1940s, he argues, "One of the rules you learn (in archeology) is, if you see a straight line, it means an artificial structure, because there are no straight lines in nature. Yet there are quite a number of such structures recorded by the cameras."

According to Sitchin, it all corroborates the Sumerian statement, to be found in his first book. "Mars served as a way station," he says, citing a 5,000-year-old Sumerian depiction and other texts (see illustration): "They say that the turn was made at Mars." He believes an ancient Mars base may have been recently reactivated which could account for the disappearance of the Russian Phobos Mars Mission as well as the U.S. Mars Observer two years ago. He also speculates that such a site may prove to be where many UFOs are now originating.

When the reporter inquired as to just what he might think of the work of de Santillana and von Dechend in *Hamlet's Mill*

(1969), Sitchin offered to kiss him on both cheeks. It seems that the two MIT professors in their great investigation of the origins of human knowledge and its transmission through myth, had raised the question: "But now, is Nibiru as important as all that?" and had gone on to answer it, "We think so. Or, to say it the other way around: once this astronomical term and two or three more are reliably settled, one can begin in earnest to get wise to and to translate Mesopotamian code."

Sitchin does not hesitate to stake his claim, "I think that I achieved it." For him it is clear, Nibiru is and remains the 12th planet.

As to when it will return to Earth's vicinity, Sitchin isn't talking. Not yet anyway.

Perhaps in a future book...

15
Artifacts in Space
by J. Douglas Kenyon

Since discovery in 1981, a gigantic and enigmatic face gazing upward from the Cydonia region of Mars has held out the tantalizing promise of scientific proof that intelligent life in the universe is not unique to Earth. Though photographed from satellite five years earlier, the face had gone officially unnoticed, so space expert Richard Hoagland (author of "The Monuments of Mars") and his associates, including many top scientists and engineers who felt anything but optimistic about the chances for an effective official follow-up, proceeded to launch their own investigation. The photos of the "Face on Mars" and an apparent complex of ruins nearby were subjected to years of exhaustive research. Utilizing the most advanced tools of scientific analysis, "The Mars Mission," as the group terms itself, has produced more than enough evidence to argue plausibly that the objects of Cydonia are not only the remains of an ancient civilization, but one possessed of a science and technology well beyond our own.

The startling possibility that such artifacts exist has created considerable public pressure to return to the red planet, and was cause for more than a little consternation in the summer of 1993 when NASA lost contact with its Mars Observer probe just as it was about to begin a detailed photographic survey which could

Reprinted from Atlantis Rising Magazine, issue #2.

have proved the issue, one way or the other.

How long now must we wait until the argument can be tested? Well, perhaps not too long after all. As it turns out, the cherished concrete evidence that man is not alone in the universe may well exist in our own back yard—relatively speaking. Within the past two years, the Hoagland group claims to have discovered in numerous NASA photographs evidence of ancient civilization on our closest neighbor, the moon. And in this case, if NASA isn't up to the verification job, Hoagland insists that he and his backers are. The result could be—sometime within the next few months—the first privately funded mission to the Moon.

If anybody can pull it off, Hoagland may be the man. For more than 25 years a recognized authority on astronomy and space exploration, Hoagland has served as a consultant for all of the major broadcast networks. Among his many valued contributions to history and science, the best remembered is probably his conception, along with Eric Burgess, of Mankind's First Interstellar Message in 1971: an engraved plaque carried beyond the solar system by the first manmade object to escape from the Sun's influence, Pioneer 10. Hoagland and Burgess originally took the idea to Carl Sagan, who successfully executed it aboard the spacecraft, and subsequently acknowledged their creation in the prestigious journal "Science." It was Hoagland who proposed the Apollo 15 experiment in which Astronaut David Scott, before a worldwide TV audience, simultaneously dropped a hammer and a falcon feather to see if it was true—as Galileo predicted—that both would land at the same time. Once again Galileo was vindicated. Since the 1981 discovery of the "Face on Mars" Hoagland had devoted most of his time to the pursuit of scientific evidence for extraterrestrial intelligence.

We caught up with him the day after Hollywood's latest space epic "Stargate" had opened nationwide to enormous audiences. Since the film deals with the idea of extraterrestrial intervention in Earth's history, we wanted to know what portents, if any, he saw. "The problem with the movie," Hoagland offered, "is that the vehicle for anything interesting isn't there after the first half-hour. It disintegrated into a kind of shoot-em-up with an awful lot of ends totally unfulfilled." But the film's quality—or lack of it—notwithstanding, Hoagland is encouraged by the public reception. "The fact that people are rushing to see this indicates to me there is almost an archetypal compulsion to know more, and if we put together the right vehicle, which we are attempting to do, we may have a ready audience."

Hoagland was alluding to a couple of possible film projects now in the talking stages based on the Mars and Moon work. The outcome, hopefully, will be both a scientific documentary and a fictionalized treatment presenting some of the more speculative aspects of the research. Such matters, though, are not his primary concern.

Uppermost in Hoagland's mind and those of his associates are recent discoveries on the moon. In clear NASA photos, some nearly 30 years old—from both manned and unmanned missions, from orbiters and landers—can be seen giant structures unexplainable by any known geology—what Hoagland calls "architectural stuff."

"In sharp contrast to the Mars data, where we have been constrained to look at two or three pictures of the Cydonia region with increasingly better technology—3D tools, color, polarametric, and geometric measurements—with the moon we are data rich. We have literally thousands, if not millions of photographs."

Yet with pictures taken from many directions and many different lighting conditions, angles and circumstances of every kind, Hoagland's team has produced "stunning corroboration" that all the photos are of the "same highly geometric, highly structural, architectural stuff." In fact, he says "In many cases, the architects on our team now are able to recognize the standard Buckminster Fuller tetrahedal truss, a hexagonal (six-sided) design, with cross bars for bracing. I mean, we're looking at standard engineering, though obviously not created by human beings." The structures appear to be very ancient, "battered to hell by meteors...it looks like it had gone through termite school. It's been motheaten and shattered and smashed by countless bombardments. The edges are soft and fuzzy because of micro meteorite abrasions like a sand blasting."

Hoagland explains that on an airless world there's nothing to impede a meteor from reaching the surface or reaching a structure on the ground. Nevertheless, "we're seeing a prodigious

THE "SHARD"
A ruined skyscraper on the Moon? This striking object has been termed "the Shard," a name deliberately chosen to imply that it could have once been part of a significantly larger feature. Photographed on film, scanned, and radioed back to Earth in February, 1967 by the NASA's unmanned Lunar Orbiter III (III-84M), the structure is a vertical, "swollen" column—casting a corresponding shadow —standing at least a mile and a half above the horizon. (The geometric cross-like feature seen above the column is a camera registration mark, placed on the film before the spacecraft left Earth.) "The Shard" is located just southwest of the Sinus Medii central region. Note carefully the geometric detail visible inside the "swollen" middle section of "the Shard." There's no plausible geological explanation for this, or any other aspect of this object.

THE "CASTLE"
This computer-enhanced photo, taken from lunar orbit near the craters Ukert and Triesnecker, is a highly enlarged section of an original NASA Apollo image, AS 10-32-4822. The mission photograph was acquired by an Apollo 10 astronaut, using a hand-held 70 mm camera, May, 1969. The highly reflective structure and background fragmentary geometric pattern are completely inexplicable by any known lunar analysis carried out by NASA. The independent scientific investigation indicates an increasing likelihood that these anomalies are in fact the product of intelligent design. The highly reflective, highly anomalous fragment in the center has been termed "the Castle." Several public versions of this photograph—including a "stereo pair" of "the Castle" and "the grid"—have been confirmed.

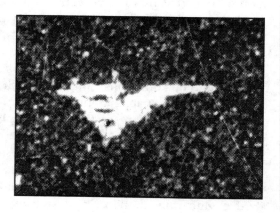

Photo credit NASA and The Mars Mission
Captions by Richard Hoagland

amount of structural material." Spread over a wide area the material is turning up at several locations. "It looks as if we're seeing fragments of vast, contained enclosures—domes, although they are not inverted salad bowls. They are much more geometric, more like the step pyramids of the Biosphere II in Arizona. We're looking at something which is extraordinarily ancient left by someone not of this earth, not of this solar system, but from someplace else."

One of the most interesting structures appears to be an enormous free-standing tower, "a crystalline glass-like partially preserved structure—a kind of a megacube—standing on remnants of a supporting structure roughly seven miles over the southwest corner of a central part of the moon called the Sinus Medii region."

If all of this exists, one of the most important questions may be: Why didn't NASA notice? If Hoagland is right, "Something funny has been going on." Indeed.

Recently Hoagland presented the Lunar material at Ohio State University. In the months since, discussions have raged on the Internet, Prodigy, Compuserve and other on-line computer services. Many questions now being put to him are coming from scientists and engineers within NASA, many of whom have had direct experience with the lunar program, yet who have been kept in the dark regarding any ET evidence. Hoagland has passed on the present state of the research and asked for input, and he's left with the inescapable impression that "something incredible has been missed."

As Hoagland sees it, there are only two possible explanations: "Either we're dealing with incredible dumbness, in which case we spent $20 billion for nothing because we went there, took photographs, came home and didn't realize what we were seeing. Or we're dealing with the careful manipulation of the many by the few." The latter may not be as implausible as it might at first sound. "If you're in a system which is cornerstoned on honesty, integrity, openness, full disclosure," he explains, "and there are folks in there who are operating contrary to those precepts, they won't get caught because no one is suspicious."

Actually Hoagland has moved beyond suspicion to belief,

and he says he can prove his point. "The smoking gun" is a report by the Brookings Institution commissioned by NASA at its inception in 1959. Entitled "Proposed Studies on the Implications of Peaceful Space Activities for Human Affairs," the study "examines the impact of NASA discoveries on American society 10, 20, 30 years down the road. On page 215 it discusses the impact of the discovery of evidence of either extraterrestrial intelligence—i.e., radio signals or artifacts left by that intelligence on some other body in the solar system. The report names three places that NASA might expect to find such artifacts—the Moon, Mars or Venus. It then goes on to discuss the anthropology, the sociology, the geo-politics of such a discovery. And it makes the astounding recommendation that for fear of social dislocation and the disintegration of society, NASA might wish to consider NOT telling the American people. It's right there in black and white. It recommends censorship. Now that's what they've been doing." Hoagland believes that anthropologist Margaret Mead, one of the authors of the report, was responsible for the recommendation, which he believes came out of her experience in American Samoa. In the 1940s Mead witnessed the devastation of primitive societies exposed for the first time to sophisticated Western civilization. "That experience so moved her, so changed her perspectives that when she examined the whole ET possibility, she projected and mapped on that experience. She basically felt that if we even learned of the existence of extraterrestrials it could destroy us, therefore people can't be told."

Believing as he does that NASA and perhaps even higher levels of government have been committed to keeping people in the dark regarding the realities of extraterrestrial intelligence, Hoagland is not very sanguine about the chances of success for such high-profile programs as SETI (Search for Extraterrestrial Intelligence). "They are a complete, absolute farce. They are a false front Western town. They do not mean what they purport to mean. They are a red herring. They are a bone to the Star Trek generation." In fact, Hoagland has become so dubious of government intentions on such matters that he suspects the entire alien abduction phenomenon is a misinformation campaign calculated to scare people off the subject. "If there has been a policy to obfuscate and confuse people on behalf of the objective data," he reasons, "what would that policy do and how far would it extend to the idea of ET contact? If you had a few real contacts with someone who was trying to give us messages and trying to lead us to new insights and the fear on the part of government structure had been that this will destroy civilization itself, would not that government also put in place a program to misinform, to confuse, to politically spin in the wrong direction those few real contacts ˈby submerging them in a sea of misinformation about contacts?"

Part of the evidence for benign extraterrestrial contact Hoagland sees in the crop circle phenomenon. "The thing that makes them different from the monuments of Mars or the ancient cities on the moon," he reasons, "is that they are occurring in the crop field here on earth and they are occurring in the present time." He sees little doubt that the circles are not of this world. "We simply do not have the technology, let alone the knowledge base, to construct the multileveled communication symbols that the crop circles represent. So that once you eliminated the hoaxers...." He chuckles, "If Doug and Dave hoaxed the circles, they deserve a Nobel prize." Hoagland resumes his thought. "The level of sophistication of the information encoded in these symbols is so vast and so congruent with the lunar and Mars work that you're forced to conclude that whoever the artists are, they know a bit more than contemporary science, and/or the media or, for.that matter, the government."

At any rate, Hoagland's group is now planning an end run around the government's monopoly on ET-related space exploration information. The time has come, he believes, for a privately funded mission to the moon. Already investors have expressed interest. "We're talking a few tens of millions of dollars, not really the price for the special effects in one major motion picture. We could go to the moon and get stunning live CCD quality color television images of the things we're seeing in these 30-year-old NASA still pictures—still frames." Such a mission, if funded, could be launched within 15 months. Using new technology and a solid fueled rocket, a 500 to 600 lb. payload could be delivered into lunar orbit where it could provide "stunning camera and telescopic live transmission capabilities." The mission could even do more science. One group has expressed interest in sending a gamma ray spectrometer designed to survey the moon for water, which in Hoagland's scenario there now has to be.

The mere possibility of such a mission may already be forcing NASA to be more open. Hoagland and other members of his group have recently received a front-door invitation to view extensive previously unreleased film archives. The bureaucracy, he feels, is already moving to cover itself and forestall the eventual embarrassment of being proved out of touch, to say the least.

PART FIVE
NEW CONNECTIONS

16
Crystal Planet
by Joseph Jochmans, Litt.D.

Is there, flowing across the landscape of our world, a single planetary energy system, long forgotten to modern humanity? And here and there along the energy pathways, did a prehistoric global civilization once tap into its power by building vast transmission and receiving stations, using various forms of monumental architecture?

Have today's historians been so out of touch with the obvious inter connections of all of these remains that they have tried to explain the silent sentinel ruins as nothing more than "primitive" construction projects having little meaning or purpose beyond localized superstitious needs?

Were such mysterious sites as Stonehenge in England, or Machu Picchu in Peru, or the Pyramids of the Sun and Moon near Mexico City, or the megalith temples of Malta, or the stone heads of Easter Island, or Serpent Mound in Ohio, or thousands upon thousands of other structures scattered across the globe, simply a matter of chance arrangement or design? Have the modern theories, whatever they may be, fallen far short of explaining what really once was?

Is it true that these great monumental edifices were deliberately fixed into the geometric configuration of an "enchanted" energy landscape? And did they, altogether, create a gigantic in-

Reprinted from Atlantis Rising Magazine, issue #7.

tricate web-like pattern, the meaning and purpose of which has defied the most scholarly of modern archaeologists and historians to fully explain? What is the missing element that interlinks everything into a single fabric and weave, of which the prehistoric linear patterns among the silent structures are but the threads?

Is there a universal energy source, once known but lost to us today, which springs from the Earth? Was it distributed along the sacred lines and pathways, and broadcast out of the temples situated at the focal points? Is this is the mythic hidden "power" of magic and healing at one time shared by everyone, in a forgotten Golden Age in the distant past? How was such a system lost, and can it be understood and restored again today?

Several modern leading researchers in the fields of ancient mysteries and earth energies have gleaned from ancient sources what may be new answers to these questions regarding the true nature of the planet and its power systems, as well as how these have affected not only climatic and geologic changes in the Earth, but also significant physical-emotional-mental-spiritual transformations among peoples and nations.

What is also being realized is that ongoing shifts and alterations in personal and planetary energy fields have subtle yet profound influences on world events. Only as we can learn more concerning earth energies how they were once used and can be rediscovered again today will we find an important key to the potential directions of the future ahead of us.

Memories of a Broken Web of Power

Among ancient and modern indigenous peoples the world over are very similar traditions of earth energy patterns and how they were once utilized. In England, alignments among standing stones and stone circles are called leys, along which flowed the life force that fertilized the landscape. In Ireland they are remembered as *fairy paths* and in Germany as *holy lines*. The Greeks knew them as the *Sacred Roads of Hermes*, while the ancient Egyptians regarded them as the *Pathways of Min*.

The Chinese today still measure the *Lung Mei* or "dragon currents" which affect the balance of the land, as practiced through the ancient art of *Feng shui* Much in the same fashion as the application of acupuncture needles in Chinese medicine helps the flow of *Chi* or life force in the human body, so the placement of pagodas, stones, trees, temples and houses in the environment was regarded as a way to "heal" the Earth.

Likewise, the Native Australians still go on walkabouts or pilgrimages down their dream *paths*, crisscrossing the desert in an effort to seasonally reenergize the life centers of the region. They work with boards called *Turingas* which map out the dream lines, and by meditating on them are able to predict the approach of storms, and the location of game animals as they interact with the line systems.

The old Polynesians spoke of using the *te lapa* or "lines of light" flowing in the ocean as a method of navigation. The stone heads of Easter Island and the sacred *Ahu* platforms of Hawaii were so positioned as to receive their *mane* or life power along *aka threads* from over the watery horizons.

When the Spanish conquistadors entered Peru in the sixteenth century, they found the entire Inca Empire organized around *wacas* or sacred centers situated along *ceque* lines which all converged at the Coriconcha or Temple of the Sun in ancient Cuzco. Similarly, the Mayas of the Yucatan interconnected their pyramid sanctuaries by means of *Sacbes* or raised white roadways that were built in dead straight segments through the jungle swamps.

In Western North America, medicine wheels and kiva circles are often found in linear arrangements, and in the Midwest and East coastal regions the Mound Builders left many of their great earthen works in alignments covering large areas. In New England mysterious stone chamber sites also fit into linear patterns, and many Native American shamans today speak of energies called *Orenda, Manitou* and by other names which flow through the Earth to promote healing.

Not only were local terrestrial powers tapped into around the world, but many ancient and modern traditions recognize that these local patterns were part of a much larger energy configuration called the Earth's Crystal Grid.

Spotted Fawns, Vibrating Balloons & Splitting Continents

The Elders of the Native American Hopi nation say that the

Earth's surface is like the back of a spotted fawn. As the fawn grows, the spots move and change number. Similarly, every time the Earth Mother "sings a new song" or enters a new vibrational shift, Her power centers also change to a new configuration, interconnected by a more complex sacred geometry.

In the 1970s several students of inventor Buckminster Fuller performed a series of experiments that were later repeated by other researchers and taken to new levels. The experiments involved submerging a balloon in a liquid medium filled with blue dye, and subjecting the balloon and liquid to a certain frequency of vibration. The result was the dye collected at specific points on the surface of the balloon, and thin lines formed joining the points in geometric arrangements. When the frequency was turned higher the original dye points first quickly dissolved and then a greater number of dye points began to slowly form, joined by lines in a more complex configuration.

It is now believed that the Earth also has its own energy centers, much like the human body has chakras and acupuncture points. Like the growing fawn or the balloon subjected to a higher frequency, when the Earth periodically moves into a higher energy state, so the overall planetary energy patterns shift into new crystallike forms. This is a global phenomenon which appears to have been going on for a very long period of time.

A study of map projections and worldwide geological patterns conducted in 1976 by Athelstan Spilhaus, consultant for the National Oceanographic and Atmospheric Administration (NOM), revealed that when the super continent Pangaea first broke apart approximately 220 million years ago forming the rudiments of our modern day continental masses, the breakup occurred along equidistant lines forming the edges and points of a *tetrahedron*. This is a geometric shape composed of four equilateral triangles, the First and simplest of the Sacred Solids of Plato.

Based on the research of Hanshou Liu of the Goddard Space Flight Center, who analyzed stress lines in the Earth caused by polar and land movements over the last 200 million years, Spilhaus found that what was next outlined in the planetary structure was a combination *cube* and *octahedron*. A Cube is composed of six squares, and the Octahedron has eight triangles arranged like two Egyptian pyramids end to end, or in the config-

uration of a flourite crystal. These constitute the next two higher
Platonic Solids beyond the Tetrahedron. The Earth's crystalline
evolution did not end there, however, but has moved into two
even more complex Platonic forms.

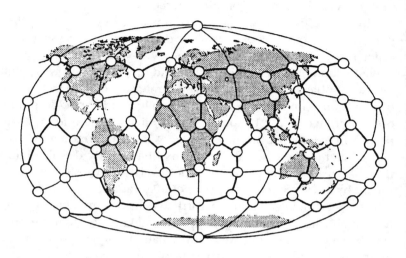

The Crystal Grid as a Key to Nature and Ancient Mysteries

In 1973, three Russian historians Nikolai Goncharov, construction engineer Vyacheslav Morozov, and electronics special-
ist Valery Makarov announced in the science journal for the So-
viet Academy of Science, *Chemistry and Life*, their discovery of
a geometric grid pattern which appears to interlink a wide number of natural phenomena into a single planetary system. Their
work was based on the findings of American researcher Ivan T.
Sanderson who identified what he called twelve "vile vortexes"
or electromagnetic energy disturbances located equidistant over
the surface of the globe, the so-called Bermuda Triangle near the
Caribbean and the Devil's Sea off Japan being two of these. What
the three Russians found was an underlying framework linking
these centers into a dual crystal structure, a combination between an *icosahedron* and a *dodecahedron.* Not surprisingly,
these happen to be the Fourth and Fifth Solids in the Platonic series, which were projected outward by the Earth for over the
last million years or so.

The Icosahedron is composed of twenty triangles forming a

ball, and the Dodecahedron is made up of twelve pentagons as its sides. When these two are distributed over the surface of the globe, their lines and node points closely delineate the following planetary elements:

1. High and low barometric pressure areas in the Earth's atmosphere, where storms originate and move along the crystal lattices.
2. The centerpoints for major ocean currents and whirlpools.
3. Areas of highest and lowest solar and electric influx, along with regions of highest and lowest geomagnetic gauss strength.
4. Points of magnetic/electric anomaly, which serve as gateways into other dimensions.
5. Major planetary fracture zones, where the tectonic plates come together and create seismic and volcanic activities.
6. Major concentrations of ores and petroleum.
7. Planetary hotspots where the internal magma surges closest to the surface.
8. Migration routes of land, air and sea creatures.
9. Locations of major life breeding grounds and genetic pool regions, where new species have originated.
10. Concentrations of human population centers, both past and present.
11. Birth places for human religions, philosophies, sciences, arts and architectural forms.

This last point is most significant, for it includes the location of most of the major ancient monuments either directly at or clustered around each of the node points of the Earth's crystal grid, including: the Great Pyramid at Giza in Egypt, the ruins of Great Zimbabwe in central Africa, the cultural center of Mohenjo Daro on the Indus river in Pakistan, the Shensi Pyramids in China, the Kunoonda stone circle complex in Australia, the ruins of Nan Madol on the Caroline Island of Pohnpei, the stone heads of Easter Island, Machu Picchu in Peru, the Pyramids of the Sun and Moon at Teotihuacan in Mexico, the Hopi Four Corners area in the American Southwest, to name only a few. Fully 3,300 separate ancient monuments or sacred complexes have been found directly associated with the Icosa Dodeca grid configuration.

Many of these same structures are also related to the more localized linear energy patterns. It would appear that the planetary crystal grid lines form the main arteries of power, while the local extensions are like capillaries running off the main system which brings the "flow" of life force into smaller regions.

That the Ancients were very familiar with the Earth's crystal grid can be seen in their literature and in their remains. Plato, in describing how the planet appeared from space, stated that it looked like a ball sewn together with twelve pieces of cloth. These would be the twelve pentagons of the Dodeca, which also forms the framework for the Icosa grid as well. Gold objects found in Khmer ruins in Southeast Asia and among Druidic remains in France, in addition to stone balls unearthed from the Neolithic period in Scotland, were all shaped to show the geometric progression of the crystal grid from Tetrahedron to Dodecahedron, and were used as teaching tools for the Initiates to understand the evolution of the planetary energy systems.

Are We in the Middle of the Next Crystal Evolution?

Within the last few years researchers around the world have been seeing that a dramatic shift has been taking place in the natural phenomena of the planet. Earthquakes are occurring where there have not been quakes before. Volcanic activity is increasing worldwide. Weather patterns and climates are in major flux, with a rise in floodings in some areas and droughts in others. Migration routes are changing, with birds nesting in new places, and dolphins and whales are increasingly beaching themselves as if lost or looking for new routes. Most significantly, the geomagnetic field of the planet has been steadily dropping, while the Schumann Resonance or overall global frequency is increasing.

Like the dye points on the balloon, a change of frequency means the old centers and the old crystal grid are dissolving, and a new crystal energy structure is in formation.

Beyond the Platonic series of Solids is another form being geometrically generated out of the old Icosa Dodeca crystal. If you take an Icosahedron and join together with lines every other point inside the form, you create twelve pentacles or five-pointed stars. If you extend the outer edges of the Icosahedron and join these node points together, you create a second group of twelve pentacles or stars. This becomes the seed crystal that gives birth to a new crystalline form called a *double penta do-decahedron*, composed of twelve double pentacles equally spaced across the surface of the globe.

In one of his prophetic visions of the future, the apostle John, writing in his *Book of Revelation*, described the coming New Jerusalem as "having the light like the light unto a crystal," and being "as long as it is wide as it is high," or geometric in shape. He described it has having "crowns." or node points, and indicated that its structure would be based on "a golden measure" or the golden mean proportion of 1 to 1.617. Significantly, the only geometric figure that is composed entirely of golden mean proportions is a five-pointed star, the pentacle. What the prophet may have been portraying is the future New Earth with the new Penta Dodeca crystal energy grid fully in place. The "twelve gemstones" and "twelve gates" of the New Jerusalem would be the twelve double pentacle faces of the Penta Dodeca crystal form.

Because the bioelectrical field of the human brain is intricately related to the geomagnetic field of the Earth, any energy shifts in the planet could cause corresponding transformations in the consciousness of humanity as a whole. Is the present spiritual awakening occurring among humankind around the world tied into the transition from one planetary crystal energy form to another? Are prophesied "earth changes" not something to be feared, but are simply signposts for both personal and planetary changes now happening, linked with the Earth's crystalline metamorphosis? Will the apostle John's vision of a coming world of universal peace and tranquility be our eventual Gift once the Earth's crystal transformations are completed? These are questions only the future will answer.

17

Geophysics and the Paradigm Shift

by Laura Lee

Do you feel like time is "speeding up"? Are you experiencing changes in your sleep patterns and dream states, alternating periods of "black hole" sleep with periods of intense and vivid dream activity? Have your emotions and relationships intensified? Is deja vu a common experience for you? What about the vague feeling that something is different now, that somehow, you've been through this before? You may be happy to discover, as I was, that you are not just imagining it. You are not alone. And there are very real reasons for these experiences.

Evidence is accumulating from diverse sources to suggest that these experiences, psychological though they may be, have a physiological and geophysical component. This means that changes within Earth's body affects our bodies, because the two are tied in subtle ways.

So subtle, in fact, that we are mostly unaware of this "bonding" until viewed in the life or fertility cycles of many species that are timed to the tides or full moon, or in the recently discovered magnetite, a specialized brain cell, found in abundance in the brains of mammals (including humans) and birds that tune and respond to Earth's magnetic field. Allowing homing pigeons to home in, sea creatures to navigate migration patterns, magnetite may also be the key to understanding why some people and

Reprinted from Atlantis Rising Magazine, issue #7.

Gregg Braden

animals are sensitive to earthquakes before they happen (they sense the localized anomalies in the magnetic field known to occur in the hours and days prior to seismic events) and perhaps why sheep have been seen to sit in rows upon ley lines, natural lines of magnetic force in the Earth. So, we are tuned and we are affected. What are the changes within the Earth affecting us?

They are cyclical, occurring in extremely long time waves, by human standards. That's one of the reasons we are mostly unaware of them. The best place to view the clues left behind by previous cycles is in geological record, the book kept by Earth herself. Science knows little about how to read these cycles, or what they mean. That information may be contained in the records of the previous cultures who lived through them.

Breakthrough research comes from Gregg Braden, who has correlated the two records and pieced together a fascinating, and, if he's right, important picture. Braden's career history and personal experiences had much to do with recognizing this new evidence. Former experience as a computer systems designer and geologist led him to recognize the evidence of these geophysical cycles in the geologic record. Two near-death experiences at an early age, and years spent guiding tours to sacred sites throughout the world, led him to research the temples, texts, myths, and traditions of various ancient cultures.

Braden found that previous cultures had not only experienced and left records of their experience of these cycles, they found them useful for easing access to higher states of consciousness. So useful, that in between cycles, they designed and built temples, or utilized natural sites that exhibit these same geophysical, cyclical conditions, the same ones that are in exponential transition on Earth today. They called this point in the cycle "The Shift of the Ages." What's more, they left us the instructions.

Geophysical Condition #1: Earth's Rising Base Frequency

Earth's background base frequency, or "heartbeat" (called Schumann resonance, or SR), is rising dramatically. Though it varies among geographical regions, for decades the overall measurement was 7.8 cycles per second. This was once thought to be a constant; global military communications developed on this frequency. Recent reports set the rate at 8.6, and climbing. Science doesn't know why, or what to make of it. Braden found data collected by Norwegian and Russian researchers on this; it's not widely reported in the U.S. (The only reference to SR to be found in the Seattle library reference section is tied to the weather. Science acknowledges SR as a sensitive indicator of temperature variations and worldwide weather conditions. Braden believes the fluctuating SR may be a factor in the severe storms, floods, and weather of recent years.)

Geophysical Condition #2: Earth's Diminishing Magnetic Field

While earth's "pulse" rate is rising, her magnetic field strength, on the other hand, is declining. According to Professor Bannerjee of the University of New Mexico, the field has lost up to half its intensity in the last 4,000 years. And because a forerunner of magnetic polar reversals is this field strength, Prof. Bannerjee believes that another reversal is due. Braden believes that because these cyclical shifts are associated with reversals, Earth's geological record indicating magnetic reversals also marks previous shifts in history. And, within the enormous time scale represented, there were many of them.

The Book of Earth Past

The geological record is like one big book whose sedimentary pages record the events of their day. Magnetic pole reversals leave their mark in the sea floor's spreading ridges; the once molten rock's iron particles aligned to the north pole as the lava cooled and hardened. Today, through core samples, we can "read" that the magnetic orientation to North shows periodic

180-degree flipping. Over a period of 76 million years, 171 reversals are recorded, nine of them in the past 4 million years. "My suspicion is that the magnetic flip-flop occurs very quickly once Earth's magnetic field has diminished near the Zero Point, then slowly builds up again," says Braden.

It may happen soon, or thousands of years from now—it's impossible to pinpoint exact dates in the geological record, says Vince Migliore, editor of Geo-Monitor Newsletter. "But we know that Earth's geomagnetic field, known to fluctuate in its intensity in the recent geologic past, is now just a fraction of what it has been historically." What is it right now, on a scale of 10, 5 being average? I asked him. The answer: 1.5! What do scientists know of the effects? According to Migliore, a common phenomenon is tremendous migration of the magnetic poles. There are reports of such magnetic anomalies, picked up by compasses, ranging up to 15 to 20 degrees away from magnetic North.

Temple Mechanics

Braden has measured many ancient temples exhibiting unusual magnetic fields and frequencies. Anecdotal reports concur: from the 1800s to the present, people have reported hearing ringing and hums, seeing strange glows, and feeling sparks from megalithic standing stones and the Great Pyramid. The latter, a mysterious and magnificent engineering feat is, according to Braden, the only known temple to exhibit both geophysical parameters of diminished magnetics and rising base frequency.

As a resident of New Mexico, Braden spends considerable time among the temples of the Southwest, and points out that what we, in this country, call "Indian ruins" are referred to as "temples" in other countries, and that influences the way we think about and care for these legacies. In the circular underground temples, called kivas, built by the Anasazi culture of a thousand years ago, Braden sees "tuned resonant cavities" for the purpose of eliciting various altered states of consciousness. A resonant cavity is a hollow space, the dimensions of which have a naturally occurring frequency which sets up a resonance, or harmonic feedback loop, and tunes with another frequency. "In the case of certain kivas," says Braden, "that other frequency is the human mind."

Visit to a Kiva

He tells the story of a tour of one well-preserved kiva, where his group was told they couldn't play Native American cedar flutes as they had in the past. "I was looking forward to experiencing the kiva's unusual acoustics and the meditative reverie that often results from it. But a park ranger met us, saying that musical instruments were now prohibited, because a few days prior, a visitor had died of a brain aneurysm while blowing a conch shell in the middle of this kiva. The park wasn't willing to risk any more accidents."

My husband Paul had a much happier experience in that very same kiva. With Braden as tour guide, Paul and I spent several days hiking dusty trails linking kivas of different dimensions (and frequencies) to outposts and rock outcroppings, some decorated with petroglyphs. Walking through a kiva, Paul stopped and stood, listening as with his inner senses. He sat down in the middle, closed his eyes, and tuned in. It was so powerful, with such intense emotional energy, he later reported, that he moved to the kiva's edge, sat on a ledge, continued his mediation, and there had an awakening that he feels changed the course of his life.

Inner Mechanics

Is it any accident that many temples and sites known as sacred offer a localized experience of less magnetics and/or higher frequency? In the Great Pyramid, the upper known chambers have significantly lower magnetic readings than the lower chambers, and significantly higher than normal frequencies have been measured.

Braden believes that this was part of the technology developed by previous cultures to recreate these conditions between cycles, in chambers especially designed to utilize them for initiations.

Just what effect does a lesser magnetic field and higher vibratory rate have on us?

"The opportunity to more easily change the patterns that can determine how and why we love, fear, judge, feel, need, and hurt," says Braden. "Dense magnetics lock in emotional and mental patterns from generation to generation in the morphogenetic field. With lesser magnetic fields, this seems to ease up, allowing easier access to higher states, as the cells of our body tune to, and try to match, Earth's rising base frequency like tuning forks, thereby raising our own."

Legacies both written and oral indicate that ancient cultures worldwide have experienced the "shifts" of previous cycles. "The ancient record keepers left us the markers for this event, what to expect, and, very importantly, a strategy for these times," says Braden. "The strategy involves making the most of the opportunity for access to higher states of consciousness, and focuses on the importance of emotions. The Essenes made a science of this. And the ancient Egyptian mystery school initiations took place in specific temples in sequence, one before the other. Each temple, and personifying temple deity, was dedicated to one aspect of the human psyche. Each aspect must be balanced prior to moving to the next level."

Initiation Rites

Why the focus on emotions? Looking through current biotech research, Braden found that our very DNA, our life codes, are affected by our emotions. The way he explains it, DNA coding options come up as 'electives' at various times, able to turn on or off. Emotions trigger specific biochemicals, which influence the chemical voltage and frequency of cells, to which molecules such as DNA respond. Therefore it is possible for our emotions to act as "switches" for "turning on" options within our DNA to make new amino acids (reports of spontaneous mutations are on the increase) in preparation for an evolutionary leap. Ancient wisdom, then, offers a successful strategy for life that works on many levels.

Earth as Global Temple

"We are living the completion of a cycle that began nearly 200,000 years ago, and a process of initiation that was demonstrated over 2,000 years ago." says Braden. "In past ages, through proper initiation, these special conditions were utilized for clearer access to higher states. Now we don't have to recreate them in specialized temple chambers. We don't have to go anywhere. We are living in a global initiation chamber, with these geophysical conditions occurring on a worldwide scale. It's as if Earth herself is preparing us for the next stage of evolution."

Science may be witnessing events for which there are few points of comparison, but, says Braden, "ancient traditions have preserved the understanding that during key moments in human history, a wisdom has been offered allowing individuals to experience rapid change without fear. This is one of those moments. This wisdom is now being passed down. Your life is preparing you for the shift. The recorded and predicted timetable is intact. The time is now."

The Chinese say, "may you live in interesting times." For those frightened of change, who equate dull with secure, this is meant as a curse. Yet interesting times, if today is any indication, may also be a rare window of opportunity, a chance to get it right this time around, a collective journey, and certainly, High Adventure. It's a personal choice.

Laura Lee hosts a nationally syndicated radio show (the Laura Lee Show).

18

Hidden Keys in
Ancient Mythology
by Laura Lee

It seems our cultural heritage is full of the greatest codes and ciphers ever written, and we're just now beginning to crack them.

Brainteaser No. 1 Look around you for a universal clock that will remain, thousands of years from now, intact, fully operational, a piece of machinery that will last for all time, that *tells* time, from any vantage point on Earth's surface. Hint: Look Up. At night. Far from the city lights. Now tell the time. (For solution, keep reading.)

Brainteaser No. 2 Now devise a means of taking a "snapshot" in time of a significant moment. Put it in a universal code, that anyone using the same clock can understand. Now preserve it so it may travel intact thousands of years into the future. Hint: This quote, "The Universe is made up of stories, not atoms" from Muriel Ruckeyser, will do nicely. (For solution, keep reading.)

Forgotten Solutions The very ancient, yet unacknowledged, culture which came up with solutions to these challenges laid the basis for traditions still in use today. As we awake from the Western society's cultural amnesia, we are piecing together the

Reprinted from Atlantis Rising Magazine, issue #8.

William Sullivan

fragments of a long-lost heritage.

The clock is Nature's own. This mechanism, provided by Earth's distinctive wobble within the solar system within the Galaxy, gives us the vantage point of sitting at the inner spring mechanism of a giant clock. It's small and large wheels within wheels are the visible planets, the constellations, and local Galactic arm, going about their orbits in relation to one another. This is how the ancients kept time, in the grandest sense.

Significant snapshots in time were recorded by a method equally ingenious: simple and entertaining stories containing precise astronomical notations. The mythmakers and astronomer-priests were one and the same, and simply watched the story's cast of characters (distinctly drawn personifications of the various planets and constellations) move about the night skies like actors on a stage. The story line would unfold as a celestial soap-opera.

Dr. William Sullivan is a cultural historian and archaeoastronomer specializing in the cultures of the Andes. He demonstrates, in his new breakthrough work, The *Secret of the Incas: Myth, Astronomy, and the War Against Time,* how myth works, on one level, as a technical language charting the passage of great cycles of time. The clever insertion of universally understood, highly technical data within a universally known, deceptively simple story becomes clear in the following version of a story known to just about every ancient culture around the world. Some consider this evidence of a worldwide flood, and there is geological evidence dating to 9,600 B.C. to support such a catastrophe. In the following Andean version of Noah's Ark, Sullivan finds another layer of meaning.

Noah's Ark: The Inca Version

A shepherd hikes high into the mountains to check his flock of llamas, finding they are not eating, but watching the stars with anticipation and anxiety. One llama tells the shepherd, "Pay close attention to what I am about to tell you. That conjunction of stars there means that the whole world is about to be destroyed by a flood." So the shepherd gathers up his family, his flock, and his seeds, and they flee to the top of the highest mountain. As the rain starts pouring down the water rises, and the various animals run up to the top of the mountain. Clinging to the very top, the waters crest and then recede. Everyone stayed high and dry, except for fox, who slipped and dipped his tail in the water. And that is why the tail of the fox is black.

"In the Aymara dialect, 'pacca' means both llama and shaman, says Sullivan. Here, fox is a specific celestial object, a constellation. And in the morning sky of A.D. 650, during the December solstice, fox had 'risen' except for his tail, which dipped down below the visible horizon, the metaphorical 'waters of the deep.'" Thus a date is matched to a specific celestial conjunction, becoming a "snapshot" in time. (see diagram, page 62)

This now hidden meaning used to be obvious. Imagine living in a society that didn't have the lights on all the time; we could see *all* the stars. Now imagine living where there is less atmosphere to obscure the viewing, at an elevation of 12,000 feet, high in the Andes. There, you feel you can reach up and touch the stars. "And the Milky Way is absolutely dazzling," says Sullivan, "so bright that the clouds of interstellar dust block out the background glow of stars in certain areas, so they appear inky black and phantomlike. To the Inca, this landscape was well-known, populated by familiar animals that moved around the sky, just as we've named our constellations. If the lights were turned off so we could actually get reacquainted with the night sky, we too could see 'Fox dipping his tail'."

This concept isn't yet obvious to academia. It's been a long, lonely, largely self-financed labor-of-love since 1974, when two key books fell in Sullivan's lap. The first was The *Roots Of Civilization*, in which the author, Alexander Marshack, tells of reading an article about a bone with scratches on it. Dissatisfied with the explanations offered, he got a sudden flash of insight that it was a record of lunar cycles. In museums all over Europe, Marshack located additional Ice Age artifacts with similar scratches, some bearing the sequential marks of waxing and waning moons through a full year. He had found 25,000-year-old calendars.

The second book, written in 1969 and ignored by academia, was *Hamlet's Mill*, (the title likens the great wheel of time to a millstone turning). Authors Santillana and von Dechend proposed that myth works as a technical language encoding extremely sophisticated astronomical observations, created prior to writing and complex mathematics, and transmitted by storytellers not necessarily understanding the technical components. Staggered by the implications, Sullivan set out to test if that were true. The Inca, he decided, were the perfect test subject.

Armed with a decryption formula, (animals are stars, topography refers to constellations, gods are planets) Sullivan searched the archives for the earliest version of Inca myths.

Then he ran computer-generated star charts backwards in time, to the skies over the Andes. Using *Skyglobe* ($20 share ware) to test the match of the skies, code, and myths, he found they "lit up the computer screen like a pin-ball machine—all the right spots at the right time, proving that these myths are constructed on many levels simultaneously, and one of those levels happens to be astronomy."

Then there was field work. "Being there in the Andes, gazing at the night sky with anyone kind enough to talk to me, I asked, 'what do you call that,' and 'do you know any stories about those stars out there?' People young and old were naming the constellations and telling me versions of stories that I later found in the Spanish chronicles, the earliest source of the Inca myths, written in the early 1500s." Myth has proven itself a tenacious carrier wave.

Watching the Heavens Tick

With an overhead clock to preoccupy you nightly, naturally you'd chart where you are in the great wheel of time's passage. That was a central preoccupation of these myths, according to Sullivan. The mechanism was that peculiar motion of our Earth known as "Precession of the Equinox."

To the ancients, the clock worked like this: Earth, set like a wobbling gyroscope, spins and rotates on a tilted axis, slowly drawing a spiral as it moves through space. The visual effect: stars and planets move about the heavens, rising above or setting below the visible horizon. Each symbol of the *zodiac* (from the Greek, meaning "dial of animals") represents one of 12 constellations, arrayed around Earth like the numbers on a clock face. The horizon at the solstice and equinox is like the hand of the clock, marking to the constellation of the "hour," or Age. One cosmic "day," or complete cycle around the clock, takes 25,920 years. At the time of Christ, the constellation Pisces was visible above the eastern horizon on the Spring Equinox; today, two thousand years later, due to precessional motion, Pisces has been replaced by the constellation Aquarius, (12 into 25,920 = 2,120 years per "Age") giving us "the Dawning of the Age of Aquarius." Such astronomical observations gave rise to the Inca's own ideas of their place in history, to the delineation of world ages, and to the metaphor 'the world is destroyed and a new one created' for continuous cycles of time.

It seems the Inca took this metaphor literally, with tragic results. "Few people realize that in 1532, when a handful of Spanish adventurers destroyed the Inca Empire, it was less than a century old, yet the heir of a tradition already 2,000 years old," says Sullivan. "The impetus behind the Inca formation was a 1437 prophecy foretelling the utter destruction of Andean civilization within five generations. Incan activities and institutions were nothing less than a comprehensive response to this bleak vision."

Holding the Gate Open

To ancient cultures the world over, the Milky Way was a river or pathway, traversed by the gods and the spirits of the ancestors to and from Earth. To the Inca, it was a "gateway" to these supernatural worlds. Due to the rhythms of precessional time, that Gateway would 'open' or 'shut' when the Milky Way fell above or below the horizon at the Solstices. That the Milky Way would no longer be visible rising at the December solstice in 1532 was a predictable astronomical event. Yet to the Inca that spelled disaster: If the Gateway shut, the spirits of their ancestors could not return to ritually renew the culture; everything would end.

Sullivan believes the Inca decided it was their duty to attempt to stop the Gateway from shutting. He explains that Andean society was organized as a template of the celestial realm on Earth. Each tribe thought itself descended from a different star or constellation. This formed the basis for peaceful co-existence among tribes. Just as each star is different but lives in fixed relation to the other, each tribe had its own identity, customs, language, homeland and lived in harmony with the other tribes. For nearly 100 years, at the December solstice, the Inca Empire sacrificed one or two children from each tribe, with the intent that the souls of those children would return to their homeland among each constellation, and beg all the stars in concert not to move about the heavens in such a way as to slam the Gateway shut.

How did this fundamentalism, or literal interpretation, take hold? "The Inca took the ancient idea 'as above, so below,' and stood it on its head," says Sullivan. "They tested the relationship between the movements of the heavens over long periods of time in human history, and events on Earth. They asked, can we enact ritual in the hope of influencing the heavens, and thereby change our history by changing the course of the stars? It was an unprecedented experiment in sympathetic magic." I wonder if the Inca set themselves up for a self-fulfilling prophecy of doom. Still, the Spaniards showed up right on time, and while it's easy to imagine the six-million strong, well-armed Inca Empire defeating instead of surrendering to Pizzaro, there was no stopping the inevitable onslaught of Western invasion. It still puzzles Sullivan that his research shows concurrence between the archeological record, major transformations in Andean society, and the rhythmic changes and accessibility of the Milky Way Gateway. "When we trace the major social transitions and developments of the Andean culture over a couple of millennia, with their interpretation of reading the stars," he says, "it fits. How do we explain that?"

Hints of a Mother Culture

Still other mysteries fill in the outlines of the mythic, lost, worldwide high civilization mentioned by so many early cultures who considered a former Golden Age the mother of their own culture. Could we read other versions of Noah's Ark, such as the Sumerian story of Gilgamesh, in similar fashion? Could the Andean preist-astronomer-mythographers have conversed, using precisely the same 'meta-language,' with a Chaldean Magi or Polynesian navigator?

Recent interviews on my nationally syndicated radio show include several researchers decoding other pieces of this same puzzle:

Carl Munck *(The Code)* found that by assigning the Prime Meridian to the the Great Pyramid at Giza, and with ancient standards of measure, various monuments around the globe "know" their grid coordinates, expressed through their own dimensions and design, encoding redundant, self-referential mathematical values (with lots of pi and phi).

Stan Tenen, (*Geometric Metaphors of Life; The Alphabet in*

our Hands) with an intuitive sense of pattern recognition, and a 20-year pursuit of the hint "try base 3," found an alphabet of hand gestures, the precursor of the Hebrew letters, based on shadowgrams of one mathematically inspired spiral slice of a toroidal shape encoded in the sequence of letters in the first line of Genesis.

Paul LaViolette (*Beyond the Big Bang*) has found within ancient Egyptian, Sumerian, Babylonian, Hindu, and Maori creation myths, as well as the symbols of astrology and the Tarot, metaphors describing the rise of matter from a non-physical matrix, recently confirmed by modern science. What's more, this ancient cosmology of 'continuous creation' better fits new data coming in from astronomical observations, computer simulation, and theoretical physics than does the Big Bang Theory. LaViolette considers it no mere coincidence that our constellation pictograms for Sagittarius and Scorpio both "point" (with a spear and a tail) to what astronomers have only recently recognized as the center of the Galaxy. It's the most energetic part of the Galaxy, and it's hidden from our view by the Milky Way's arm.

Robert Bauval (*The Orion Mystery*) discovered the ancient Egyptians were building 'heaven on earth' with the Nile as the Milky Way, and the three Giza pyramids cast as the three stars of Orion's belt. Bauval and Graham Hancock (*Fingerprints of the Gods*) expand on this work (*The Message of the Sphinx*) to find evidence that this same ancient, technical language formed the basis of the architecture, cosmology, and mythology of ancient Egypt. They wound the clock of the heavens back in time to find the Sphinx, a lion, is an astronomical marker for 10,500 B.C. This date is corroborated by Geologist Robert Schoch and Egyptologist John Anthony West's work in identifying, in addition to wind erosion, the extreme erosion *by precipitation* of the Sphinx, significant because the last time the Sahara Desert saw heavy rainfall was over 9,000 years ago. (*The Mystery of the Sphinx*)

"It's more difficult to find an early culture that did *not* participate in this tradition," says Sullivan. This language is so sophisticated and idiosyncratic, it's hard to believe it was independently cooked up in different places. In all the world's great traditions, and that includes those native to North and South America, this is the cultural package, the body of ideas that created civilization."

The irony of Spanish conquistadors traveling to a neighboring continent to destroy a foreign civilization, not realizing it was a branch off the same trunk as their own, is not lost on Sullivan. That common heritage is still denied. He cites the example of one early Spanish chronicler who reported that the Andean characterizations of the planets closely matched those of the Greek and Roman (Mars = god of War; Venus = goddess of Love). It was distrusted and ignored, so fanciful and inexplicable seemed the match. Consequently, scholars today believe the Inca had no names for the visible planets save Venus. Hard to believe of a culture with a rich heritage of megalithic monuments, ancient 'machinery' that both calculated astronomical observations, and enshrined in their very design ratios and proportions so significant, so expressive of Nature's secret inner workings, its geometry is regarded as sacred. "If mythology is the 'software,' concludes Sullivan, "megalithic monuments are the hardware." With software in hand, the next quest is to log onto that megalithic hardware. Who says computers need to be built of silicon and plastic?

PART SIX
SEARCHING FOR OUR
FORGOTTEN PAST

19

Top 10 Ancient Civilizations with Advanced Technology
by David Hatcher Childress

When it comes to questions regarding such things as possibly advanced technology in ancient times or the actual physical location of the fabled lost civilization of Atlantis, the answers usually depend on with whom you are speaking. Everyone seems to have favorite candidates for which a convincing case can be made.

In his *Lost Cities* series, real-life 'Indiana Jones', David Hatcher Childress has written prolifically about ancient civilizations, and his life-long quest for their remains in some of the most remote and dangerous places of the world. Lately he has become something of a regular on national television with appearances on Fox-TV's *Sighting & Encounters*, *Discovery*, and *A&E*, as well as the NBC specials *Atlantis* and *The Mysterious Origins of Man*. Here Childress offers his 'Top 10' list of Ancient Civilizations with advanced technology.

1. Ancient Mu or Lemuria
According to various esoteric sources, the first civilization arose 78,000 years ago on the giant continent known as Mu or Lemuria and lasted for an astonishing 52,000 years. It is sometimes said to have been destroyed in earthquakes generated by a "pole shift" which occurred some 26,000 years ago, or at ap-

Reprinted from Atlantis Rising Magazine, issue #1.

proximately 24,000 B.C.

While Mu did not reach as high a technology, supposedly, as other later civilizations, it is, nevertheless, said to have attained some advanced technology, particularly in the building of long-lasting megalithic buildings that were able to withstand earthquakes. However, it was the science of government that is sometimes said to have been Mu's greatest achievement.

Supposedly, there was one language and one government. Education was the keynote of the Empire's success, and because every citizen was versed in the laws of the universe and was given thorough training in a profession or trade, magnificent prosperity resulted. A child's education was compulsory to the age of 21 in order for him to be eligible to attend citizenship school. This training period lasted for seven years; so the earliest age at which a person could become a citizen of the empire was 28.

2. Ancient Atlantis

It is said that when the continent of Mu sank, the oceans of the world lowered drastically as water rushed into the newly formed Pacific Basin. The relatively small islands which had existed in the Atlantic during the time of the Lemurian civilization were left high and dry by the receding ocean. The newly emerged land joined the Poseid Archipelago of the Atlantic Ocean to form a small continent. This continent is called Atlantis by historians today, though its real name was Poseid.

Atlantis is believed to have taken technology to very advanced stages, well beyond what exists on our planet today. In the book *A Dweller on Two Planets*, first dictated in 1884 by "Phylos the Thibetan" to a young Californian named Frederick Spencer Oliver, as well as in a 1940 sequel, *An Earth Dweller Returns*, there is mention of such inventions and devices as air conditioners to overcome deadly and noxious vapors; airless cylinder lamps, tubes of crystal illuminated by the "night side forces"; electric rifles, guns employing electricity as a propulsive force (rail-guns are similar, and a very new invention); mono-rail transportation; water generators, an instrument for condensing water from the atmosphere; and the Vailx, an aerial ship governed by forces of levitation and repulsion.

The "sleeping clairvoyant," Edgar Cayce, in a reading spoke

of the use of "aeroplanes" and of crystals or "firestones" used for energy and related applications. He also speaks of the misuse of power and warnings of destruction to come.

3. Rama Empire of India

Fortunately, the ancient books of India's Rama Empire have been preserved, unlike those of China, Egypt, Central America and Peru. Many of these ancient nations are now either desert wastelands, swallowed by thick jungle or literally at the bottom of some ocean. Yet India, despite devastation by wars and invasion, managed to maintain a large part of its ancient history.

For a long time, Indian civilization was not believed to date from much earlier than about 500 B.C., only about 200 years prior to Alexander the Great's invasion of the subcontinent. In the past century, however, the extremely sophisticated cities of Mohenjo Daro ("Mound of the Dead") and Harappa have been discovered in the Indus Valley of modern-day Pakistan.

The discoveries of these cities forced archaeologists to push the dates for the origin of Indian civilization back thousands of years. A wonder to modern-day researchers, the cities were highly developed and caused leading archaeologists to believe that they were conceived as a whole before they were built: a remarkable early example of city planning. Even more remarkable is that the plumbing-sewage system throughout the large city is superior to that found in Pakistan, India, and most Asian countries today.

4. Osirian Civilization of the Mediterranean

It is said that at the time of Atlantis and Rama, the Mediterranean was a large and fertile valley. This ancient civilization, pre-dating dynastic Egypt, was known as the Osirian Civilization. The Nile river came out of Africa, as it does today, and was called the River Stix. However, instead of flowing into the Mediterranean Sea at the Nile Delta in northern Egypt, it continued into the valley, and then turned westward to flow in the deepest part of the Mediterranean Valley where it created a large lake and then flowed out between Malta and Sicily, and south of Sardinia into the Atlantic at Gibraltar (the Pillars of Hercules). When Atlantis was destroyed in a cataclysmic upheaval, this cataclysmic change in the Atlantic slowly flooded the Mediterranean Basin, destroying the Osirian's great cities and forcing them to move to higher ground. This theory helps explain the strange megalithic remains found throughout the Mediterranean.

It is an archaeological fact that there are more than 200 known sunken cities in the Mediterranean. Egyptian civilization, along with the Minoan and Mycenean in Crete and Greece are, in theory, remnants of this great, ancient culture. The civilization built huge earthquake-proof megalithic structures and had electricity and other conveniences common during the time of Atlantis. Like Atlantis and Rama, they had airships and other modes of transport, often electrical in nature. The mysterious cart tracks of Malta, which go over cliffs and under water, may well be part of some ancient Osirian "tram-line," possibly taking quarried stone to cities that are now submerged.

Probably the best example of the high technology of the Osirians is the amazing platform found at Ba'albek, Lebanon. The main platform is composed of the largest hewn rocks in the world, the famous ashlars of Ba'albek. Some of the individual stones are 82 feet long and 15 feet thick and are estimated to weigh between 1,200 and 1,500 tons each!

5. Uiger Civilization of the Gobi Desert

Many ancient cities are said to have existed at the time of Atlantis and Rama in the Uiger civilization of the Gobi Desert. Though the Gobi is now a parched land-licked desert, these cities were ocean ports. Edgar Cayce once said that elevators would be discovered in a lost city in the Gobi Desert, and while this has not happened yet, it is not out of the question.

Vimanas and other advanced devices are said to have been in use in the Uiger area, and the famous Russian explorer Nicholas Roerich reported seeing a flying disc over northern Tibet in the 1930s. Perhaps the craft was an ancient vimana coming from a still active city using Uiger technology that exists in Northern Tibet or the Gobi Desert.

Significantly, it is claimed that the Elders of Lemuria, known as the "Thirteenth School," moved their headquarters prior to the cataclysm to the uninhabited plateau of Central Asia that we now call Tibet. Here they supposedly established a library and school known as "The Great White Brotherhood."

For instance, the great Chinese Philosopher Lao Tzu, born in 604 B.C., talked frequently of "Ancient Masters" and their profound wisdom. He wrote the famous book, Tao Te Ching, probably the most popular book ever written in Chinese. When he finally left China, near the close of his very long life, he journeyed to the west to the legendary land of Hsi Wang Mu. According to the ancient Chinese, this was the headquarters of the "Ancient Ones." Could this have been The Great White Brotherhood and the Thirteenth School of Mu?

6. Tiahuanaco

As in Mu and Atlantis, construction in South America was on megalithic scale with polygonal construction techniques designed to make the massive walls earthquake-proof. Earthquake-resistant walls were important all around the Ring-of-Fire, ancient Mu.

Homes and communal buildings were built out of megalithic blocks of stone. Because of the high regard the culture had for the well being of future generations and the value they placed upon the gradual, sustained growth of the community, structures were built to last for thousands of years. A house built of cement, wood and plaster-wall will last a hundred years or so, if kept up. Witness the megalithic construction of Egypt, Malta, Peru. These buildings are still standing today. Cuzco, the ancient capital of Peru, which was probably built before the Incas, is still inhabited today after thousands of years. Indeed, most of the buildings of downtown Cuzco today incorporate walls that are many hundreds of years old (whereas more recent buildings constructed by the Spanish are already crumbling).

Only a few hundred miles to the south of Cuzco lie the fantastic ruins of Puma Punku, high in the Altiplano of Bolivia. The ruins of Puma Punku, about one mile from the famous ruins of Tiahuanaco, are massive megalithic constructions that are tossed about like toy building blocks. What kind of cataclysmic upheaval could have done such a thing? Here is the kind of megalithic construction meant to last for thousands of years, yet, the 100-ton blocks have been torn asunder by mighty geological forces.

It would appear that the South American continent was suddenly and violently thrust upward during some kind of cataclysm, most likely a pole shift. A former sea-level canal can now be seen at 13,000 feet in the Andes Mountains. As possible evidence for this scenario, many ocean fossils can be found near Lake Titicaca. The lake is even inhabited by the only known fresh water sea horses.

7. The Mayans

Mayan pyramids are found from Central America to as far away as the Indonesian island of Java. The pyramid of Sukuh, on the slopes of Mount Lawu near Surakarta in central Java is an amazing temple with stone stelae and a step pyramid that would match any in the jungles of Central America. The pyramid is in fact virtually identical to the pyramids found at the ancient Mayan site at Uaxactun, near Tikal.

The ancient Mayans were brilliant astronomers and mathematicians whose early cities lived in agrarian harmony with earth. They built canals and hydroponic garden cities throughout the ancient Yucatan Peninsula. Some of the Mayan glyphs were allegedly radionic-type insect control devices that broadcast an "etheric vibration" of the targeted pest.

Edgar Cayce mentions the Mayas and their technology in one reading: "As for a description of the manner of construction of the stone: we find it was a large cylindrical glass (as would be termed today); cut with facets in such manner that the capstone on top of it made for centralizing the power or force that concentrated between the end of the cylinder and the capstone itself. As indicated, the records as to ways of constructing same are in three places in the earth, as it stands today: in the sunken portion of Atlantis, or Poseidia, where a portion of the temples may yet be discovered under the slime of ages of sea water—near what is known as Bimini, off the coast of Florida. And (secondly) in the temple records that were in Egypt, where the entity acted later in cooperation with others towards preserving the records that came from the land where these had been kept. Also (thirdly) in records that were carried to what is now Yucatan, in America, where these stones (which they know so little about) are now—during the last few months—being uncovered."

It is believed that an ancient Hall of Records resides somewhere in the Mayan region, probably beneath an existing pyramid complex, in an underground tunnel and chamber system. Some sources say that this repository of ancient knowledge is kept in quartz crystals that are of exceptional quality and capable of holding large amounts of information in the similar manner as a modern CD.

8. Ancient China

Ancient China, known as Han China, is said to have come, like all civilizations, from the huge Pacific continent Mu. The ancient Chinese are known for their sky-chariots, their geomancy, and the jade manufacture that they shared with the Mayas. Indeed, the ancient histories of the Chinese and the Mayas seem indelibly linked.

Anthropologists makes a good case for a Taoist influence coming to Central America by showing Shang dynasty symbols and motifs (the yin-yang is the most famous, but there are many more) and then relating them to known Mayan art and sculpture. Jade was of particular importance to the Shang Chinese. So far, the source of Chinese jade has not been pinpointed. Much of it may have come from Central America. Even the source of Central American jade is a mystery; many ancient jade mines are believed to be still undiscovered. Anthropologists suggest that Chinese voyages to Mexico, between 500-300 B.C., may have been related to Taoist trade in magic mushrooms or "drugs of longevity."

The ancient Chinese are often said to be the originators of every invention from toilet paper, earthquake detectors, paper money, canons, rocket technology, printing methods, and thousands of other clever and "high-tech" items. In 1959 archaeologists in China discovered belt buckles made out of aluminum thousands of years ago. Aluminum is generally processed from bauxite with electricity!

9. Ancient Ethiopia & Israel

From such ancient texts as the Bible and the Ethiopian book *Kebra Negast*, we have tales of the high technology of ancient Ethiopia and Israel. The temple at Jerusalem is said to have been founded upon three gigantic ashlar blocks of stone similar to those at Ba'albek, Lebanon. Today, the revered Temple of Solomon and Muslim Dome of the Rock mosque exist on this site, whose foundations apparently reach back to the Osirian civilization.

Like much of the later Phoenician construction, the building at the Temple to hold the Ark of the Covenant and the temples in Ethiopia are the last of the megalithic stone constructions. The massive Temple Mount, built by King Solomon on the ruins of an earlier megalithic temple, was made to house the ancient relic known as the Ark of the Covenant.

The Ark of the Covenant is said to have been an electrical generator box which housed several sacred objects, including a solid gold statue from earlier cultures that is called the Holy of Holies. This box and gold statue were said to have been removed from the King's Chamber in the Great Pyramid in Egypt by Moses during the period of the Exodus.

Many scholars believe that the Ark of the Covenant, as well as other ancient artifacts, were actually electrical devices, some of which were worshipped in temples as oracles. The Bible recounts how certain unauthorized persons would touch the Ark and be electrocuted.

10. The Aroi Sun Kingdom of the Pacific

The last of my list of ancient civilizations is that of the virtually unknown ancient culture of the Aroi Sun Kingdom of the Pacific. While the so-called lost continent of Mu sank over 24,000 years ago in a pole shift, the Pacific was later repopulated by a racial mixture of all civilizations, coming from Rama, China, Africa and the Americas.

An advanced island nation, with larger areas of land than are currently in the Pacific, grew up around Polynesia, Melanesia and Micronesia. Ancient legends in Polynesia attribute this remarkable civilization to the Aroi Kingdom that existed many thousands of years before the European rediscovery of the Pacific. The Aroi allegedly built many of the megalithic pyramids, platforms, arches, roads and statues throughout the central Pacific.

When some of the more than 400 gravel hills on New Caledonia were excavated in the 1960s, cement columns of lime and

Easter Island

shell matter were carbon dated by Yale and the New Caledonia Museum as having been made before 5120 B.C. and 10,950 B.C. These weird cement columns can be found in the southern part of New Caledonia and on the Isle of Pines.

According to the Easter Islanders, the statues of the islands "walked" or levitated in order to move in a clock-wise spiral around the island. On the island of Pohnpei, the Micronesians claim that the stones of the eleven-square-mile city were levitated into place.

The Polynesians of New Zealand, Easter Island, Hawaii and Tahiti all believe that their ancestors had the ability of flight and would travel through the air from island to island. Was this the Air Atlantis flight that stopped in Malta, Ba'albek, and Rama destined for the remote but popular convention center at Easter Island?

20

Top 10 Possible Locations for Atlantis

by David Hatcher Childress

A s for the best location in which to find the physical remains of Atlantis—whether in Antarctica or the Aegean, the Bahamas or the North Atlantic— intriguing clues are to be found everywhere, and sorting it all out can be confusing. In his latest book, *Lost Cities of Atlantis, Ancient Europe & the Mediterranean*, David Hatcher Childress' search for obscure evidence has turned up a vast array of fascinating material previously unavailable from any single source. Here Childress tries to bring a little order to the subject with another 'Top 10' list. Some of these choice are listed in his book and some are not.

1. Azores

Plato quoting Egyptian Priests through his uncle Solon says that Atlantis was beyond the Pillars of Hercules, fought a war with the ancient Mediterraneans, and sank in 9,400 B.C. Atlantis was a land of great seafarers, many elephants and a large plain with a gigantic harbor city of concentric circles. Because Atlantis was said to be a large island in the true ocean that surrounds the continents, it was thought to be in the mid-Atlantic. Atlantis was said to have colonized much of the world and fought a war with Greece and the Eastern Mediterranean. Its sinking left only a few scattered islands, it is believed, islands such as the Azores.

Reprinted from Atlantis Rising Magazine, issue #8.

2. Sahara

The Sahara Desert, usually the Tassili and Ahaggar Mountains in southern Algeria, Tunisia or both, has been proposed as the actual site for Atlantis. When the French colonized North Africa they soon discovered a lost world existed in southern Algeria and that the ancient harbor of Carthage was an exact miniature of the capital of Atlantis as described by the Egyptian priests, novels such as *Atlantide* (1923) were popular in France, promoting the idea of Atlantis in the Sahara. The Sahara, however, did not vanish beneath the ocean, but rather dried up and became a sandy seabed. Does Atlantis lie beneath the drifting sands and strange stone formations of the Sahara Desert?

3. Malta

Malta has huge ancient structures that are now dated as 9000 years old or older and are said by orthodox archaeologists to be the oldest stone ruins in the world. Malta is now a small rocky island that once had elephants and shows evidence of having been destroyed in a huge cataclysmic wave. Joseph Ellul and others have proposed that Malta was part of a great civilization of the past, possibly Atlantis. Malta was probably connected to other parts of the Mediterranean when a huge wave from the Atlantic filled the Mediterranean, causing the Biblical Flood. Was Malta Atlantis? The island is far too small to have been Atlantis, but it shows that the Mediterranean was a very different place 12,000 years ago.

4. Bimini

With the discovery in 1968 of what appeared to be a huge polygonal stone road in the shallow water off Bimini, Atlantis was thought to have been found in the Caribbean. A lost pyramid, underwater staircases, fallen pillars, all seemed sunken ruins indeed. Atlantis could have spread over a large portion of the Atlantic, from the Azores to the Bahamas and possibly even Florida. Recently, Indiana archaeologist Jackson Judge has suggested that Portsmouth, Ohio was the site of Atlantis.

5. South America

Because of the gigantic ruins in Peru and Bolivia and the

Massive ruins at Machu Pichu

evidence that Tiahuanaco was destroyed in a cataclysm. South America has been proposed as the site of Atlantis by number of early writers, including the British colonel Percy Fawcett, who vanished in the jungles of Brazil in 1925 while searching for a lost city of Atlantis. South America does have huge ruins and is across the Atlantic, but it seems to have risen from sea level, rather than sinking into the ocean.

6. Antarctica

When Charles Hapgood resurrected the Pin Ri'is map, a map copied from older maps by a Turkish admiral and which showed Antarctica as an ice-free continent, the concept of Atlantis in the frozen polar wasteland was born. Since Atlantis may have been destroyed in a pole shift, Antarctica was probably at a more temperate climate 10,000 years ago, and may hold megalithic ruins such as South America. Antarctica seems a long way away from the Mediterranean with which it fought a war. Also Atlantis supposedly sank beneath the ocean in a day and night. Antarctica rather accumulated ice for thousands of years. Does Atlantis lie beneath the Antarctic ice?

7. Canary Islands

While no ancient ruins have ever been discovered in the Azores, the mountaintops of the mid-Atlantic ridge, ancient ruins have been discovered in the Canary islands off the coast of Morocco. The native Guanche people of the Canaries had no knowledge of-boats when first discovered by Spanish explorers, circular stone ruins have been found on the islands, leading some to propose that the Canaries are a remnant of ancient Atlantis.

8. North Sea

The shallow areas of the North Sea off Holland, Germany, England and Scandinavia have been proposed as the site of a sunken civilization that may have been Atlantis. The Oera Linda Book discovered in Holland in the 1700s spoke of a sunken land off the Frisian islands of Holland. Jugen Spanuth, a German Pastor, took photos of underwater ruins off northern Germany in the early 1950s. Recently, researcher Paul Dunbavin has proposed that the citadel of Atlantis was located underwater between Wales and Ireland, this area being the "Plain of Atlantis" as described by Plato. Major Dutch cities like Amsterdam and Rotterdam are 40 feet or more below sea level even as you read this. They may well be the sunken cities of near future.

9. Middle East

The Middle East and Arabia has some of the largest and most baffling stone ruins in the world. The largest stone blocks in the world are to be found at Ba'albek in Lebanon. They weigh an amazing 2,000 tons each and are worthy of Atlantean architecture. Similarly, it is said that the Temple Wall in Jerusalem also has a foundation of gigantic stones, similar to Ba'albek. Recent authors such as Stan Deyo have suggested that Saudi Arabia, with its strange ruins in the central deserts, is the site of ancient Atlantis. Port cities can be found in the interior of Arabia, and while it is clear that Arabia and the Middle East have many lost civilizations to be discovered, this is obviously not a sunken area at all. The Biblical Flood did sweep over the Middle East at some time in prehistory. Did it destroy Atlantis, or did Atlantis cause the catastrophe?

10. Thera & Crete

According to the tourist literature in Greece, the explosion of the Aegean island of Thera destroyed Crete and at the same time, Atlantis. While Plato is quite explicit in his time frame and location for Atlantis (9,400 B.C. and in the Atlantic), Greek archaeologists seem certain that Atlantis can be found only a few hundred miles from Athens. Thousands of tourists come to Thera every year and drink the local Atlantis wine while they discuss Atlantis. For them, Atlantis will never be found anywhere else.